SECOND

advice to those who stutter

THE
STUTTERING
FOUNDATION®

PUBLICATION NO. 0009

www.stutteringhelp.org
www.tartamudez.org

advice to those who stutter

Publication No. 0009

Second Edition—1998
Third Printing—2003
Fourth Printing—2005

Published by

Stuttering Foundation of America
3100 Walnut Grove Rd., Suite 603
P. O. Box 11749
Memphis, Tennessee 38111-0749

Library of Congress Catalog Card Number: 98-060375
ISBN 0-933388-39-X

The Stuttering Foundation of America is a nonprofit
charitable organization dedicated to the prevention
and treatment of stuttering.

preface

In 1972, the Stuttering Foundation of America published *To the Stutterer*. Chapters were contributed by 23 people with a final summary submitted by Charles Van Riper. Each of the contributors had personally experienced a significant problem with stuttering, each of them had worked to successfully manage their stuttering problem, and each had the self-confidence to make a contribution to their fellow "brothers and sisters of the tangled tongue." This original edition has now been reprinted seven times and has been translated into several foreign languages.

Now, here we are more than thirty years later, embarking on a second edition. What an undertaking! Many of the original contributors are now deceased. Those who are still living were asked either to write an updated chapter or give permission to reprint their original chapter. The four original contributors who wrote new chapters include Joseph Agnello, Richard Boehmler, Hugo Gregory and J. David Williams. Gerald Moses and Fred Murray made only minimal changes in their original chapters.

The ten new contributors to the current edition each have a story to tell. They reflect upon their own personal histories with stuttering, and they reflect upon the clinical work they have done with others who stutter. Each contributor has captured the essence of their clinical thinking and condensed it into short, readable chapters of approximately 2,000 words. As editor, I applaud them for their ability to reduce scores of pages down to the "bare essentials" and realize that there is much more that could have been said. I appreciate their understanding.

Times have changed since 1972 when I edited the first edition of *To the Stutterer*. Back then we corresponded by telephone and U.S. Mail. My wife and I retyped all the chapters, and did so many times. I kept track not only of the costs of postage and paper, but also the costs of typewriter ribbons. For the 1998 version of *Advice To Those Who Stutter,* things were different. We corresponded via e-mail, and I managed to use only one ink jet cartridge.

Those of you who read this book will live vicariously through the experiences of the contributors. I am personally honored to have known most of the contributors to the 1972 edition of *To the Stutterer.* I am honored to know all of the contributors to this new edition of *Advice To Those Who Stutter.* I consider them to be my good colleagues and friends, and I thank them for allowing me the honor, privilege and responsibility to edit and help nurture their work.

Stephen B. Hood, Ph.D.

original foreword

from 1972

This is a remarkable book of therapy advice. Nothing like it has ever been published before. What makes it unique and unusual is that every article in this book has been written by men and women who stutter themselves. Each one of them has been 'through the mill' and knows what it is to have experienced the fear, anxiety and despair which is so often the lot of the stutterer. They know your problem.

Also all of the authors of these articles are now or have been speech pathologists. This means that they are experienced and trained in helping others with their speech problems—and they have written these articles to help you deal effectively with your stuttering.

They represent a most distinguished array of authority and prestige in the field of stuttering. Included among them are sixteen who are or have been university professors of speech pathology, six who are or have been heads of speech pathology departments in such institutions, twelve who are or have been directors of speech and hearing clinics, and they include one psychiatrist, nine Fellows of the American Speech-Language-Hearing Association, and nine authors of books on the therapy of stuttering.

Although these writers do not all agree as to exactly what you should do to overcome your difficulty, there is a lot of uniformity in their recommendations and in their thinking. We believe that their ideas will help you. We are publishing this book in your interest and hope that you will make use of it.

Malcolm Fraser
Stuttering Foundation of America

contents

CHAPTER   PAGE

preface iii

original foreword v

1   express yourself or go by freight 1
     Lon L. Emerick, Ph.D.
     Northern Michigan University, Marquette*

2   managing your stuttering *versus*
     your stuttering managing you 7
     Dorvan H. Breitenfeldt, Ph.D.
     Eastern Washington University

3   stuttering: what you can do about it 13
     Margaret Rainey, M.A.
     Shorewood Public Schools, Wisconsin*

4   two sides of the coin 19
     Hugo H. Gregory, Ph.D.
     Northwestern University, Evanston, Illinois

5   advice for persons who stutter:
     what you can do to help yourself 25
     Lois A. Nelson, Ph.D.
     University of Wisconsin, Madison

6   message to a stutterer 31
     Joseph G. Sheehan, Ph.D.
     University of California, Los Angeles*

7   toward freer speech 36
Frederick P. Murray, Ph.D.
University of New Hampshire, Durham*

8   overcoming fear and tension in stuttering 41
James L. Aten, Ph.D.
University of Denver*

9   don't ever give up! 46
Peter R. Ramig, Ph.D.
University of Colorado, Boulder

10   basic goals for a person who stutters 52
J. David Williams, Ph.D.
Northern Illinois University

11   some suggestions for adult stutterers
who want to talk easily 57
Dean E. Williams, Ph.D.
University of Iowa*

12   suggestions for self-therapy for stutterers 62
Margaret M. Neely, Ph.D.
Baton Rouge Speech and Hearing Foundation—Louisiana*

13   self-improvement after unsuccessful treatments 67
Henry Freund, M.D.
Milwaukee, Wisconsin

14   some helpful attitudes
underlying success in therapy 72
Harold L. Luper, Ph.D.
University of Tennessee*

15   message to adult stutterers 77
Gerald R. Moses, Ph.D.
Eastern Michigan University*

16 some suggestions for gaining and
    sustaining improved fluency 82
    David A. Daly, Ph.D.
    University of Michigan

17 change: potential qualities
    become actualities 88
    Joseph G. Agnello, Ph.D.
    University of Cincinnati

18 four steps to freedom 95
    Richard M. Boehmler, Ph.D.
    University of Montana, Missoula

19 recovery journal 101
    Bill Murphy, M.A.
    Purdue University

20 face your fears 107
    Sol Adler, Ph.D.
    University of Tennessee*

21 attacking the iceberg of stuttering:
    icepicks, axes, and sunshine! 111
    Larry Molt, Ph.D.
    Auburn University

22 finding your own path
    without professional help 117
    Walter H. Manning, Ph.D.
    University of Memphis

23 guidelines 124
    Paul E. Czuchna M.A.
    Western Michigan University*

24 knowledge, understanding, and acceptance 129
    Robert W. Quesal, Ph.D.
    Western Illinois University

25 maintaining dignity while
    living with stuttering 135
    Gary J. Rentschler, Ph.D.
    S.U.N.Y., Buffalo

26 your life is too important to
    spend it worrying about stuttering 141
    Kenneth O. St. Louis, Ph.D.
    University of West Virginia

27 do-it-yourself kit for stutterers 147
    Harold B. Starbuck, Ph.D.
    State University College, Geneseo, New York*

28 putting it together 151
    Charles Van Riper, Ph.D.
    Western Michigan University*

    appendix a 156

*Affiliation at the time chapter was written.

express yourself or go by freight

Lon L. Emerick

One score and seven years ago, in a desperate attempt to cure their son's chronic speech problem, my parents spent their meagre savings to send me to a commercial school for stammering. Alas, to their dismay and my deepening feeling of hopelessness, it was just another futile attempt. While I rode woefully toward home on the train, a kindly old gray-haired conductor stopped at my seat and asked my destination. I opened my mouth for the well-rehearsed "Detroit" but all that emerged was a series of muted gurgles; I pulled my abdominal muscles in hard to break the terrifying constriction in my throat—silence. Finally, the old man peered at me through his bifocals, shook his head and, with just the trace of a smile, said, "Well, young man, either express yourself or go by freight."

The conductor had shuffled on down the aisle of the rocking passenger car before the shock waves swept over me. Looking out the window at the speeding landscape through a tearful mist of anger and frustration, I felt the surreptitious glances of passengers seated nearby; a flush of crimson embarrassment crept slowly up my neck and my head throbbed with despair. Long afterwards I remembered the conductor's penetrating comment. For years I locked that and other stuttering wounds and nursed my wrath to keep it warm, dreaming that someday I would right all those unrightable wrongs. But in the end his pithy pun changed my life. The old man, incredibly, had been right.

Why indeed go by freight? Why carry excess baggage, endure endless delays, languish forgotten and rejected in sooty siding yards, be bombarded with countless jolts and unplanned stops? Why let your journey through life be dictated by the time table of stuttering? Perhaps you too are searching for some way out of a morass of jumbled box cars and the maze of tracks that seem to lead only to empty, deadened spurs. Although it is difficult to give advice without seeing you and identifying your particular situation, I do know there are several things that have helped me and many other stutterers. May I extend this challenge to you: I invite you to do something difficult but with a sweet reward—to change the way you talk. The pathway to better speech is fraught with blind alleys, dark frightening tunnels and arduous climbs. Beware of any treatment that plumes itself in novelty and promises no pain; deep inside you know this cannot work. May I show you the trail?

> Why let your journey through life be dictated by the time table of stuttering?

The first thing you must do is admit to yourself that you need to change, that you really want to do something about the way you presently talk. This is tough but your commitment must be total; not even a small part of you must hold back. Don't dwell longingly on your fluency in the magical belief that someday your speech blocks will disappear. There is no magic potion, no pink pill that will cure stuttering. Don't sit around waiting for the right time, for an inspiration to come to you—*you must go to "it."* You must see that the old solutions, the things you have done to help yourself over the years (and those cover-up suggestions from well-meaning amateur therapists, "Think what you want to say," "Slow down," etc.) simply do not work. Ruts wear deep, though, and you will find it difficult to change; even though the way you presently talk is not particularly pleasant, it is familiar. It is the unknown from which we shrink.

You must be willing to endure temporary discomfort, perhaps even agony, for long range improvement. No one, except perhaps the quack, and there are still a few around, is promising you a rose garden. Why not take the time and effort now for a lifetime of freedom from your tangled tongue? How can you do that? You break down the global problem of stuttering into its smaller parts and then solve them one at a time. It's *simple*. No one said it was *easy*. Shall we begin?

> You must be willing to endure temporary discomfort, perhaps even agony, for long range improvement

1. Are you acquainted with your stuttering pattern? What do you *do* when you stutter? What can you *see, hear* and *feel*? Where are the triggers for those sticky blocks or runaway repetitions? How does your moment of stuttering progress from the first expectation you are going to stutter until the word is uttered? How do you release a block...an extra surge of energy, a sudden jerk of your head? I am asking you to observe closely what you do when you stutter; you can use a mirror, a tape recorder, your finger tips to search for areas of tension. A friend or relative whom you trust can also help you make a careful inventory. Stuttering is not some mysterious beast that takes over your mouth—even though it may appear that way because it seems to occur so automatically. Stuttering is a series of activities that you *do*. It is your way of talking for now. Before you can change what you do, obviously you have to spend some time cataloging precisely what it is you do. Here is how one stutterer described his stuttering pattern:

Can tell when I'm going to stutter...at least three words ahead. Tense my lower jaw. Purse my lips tightly...even when trying to say the /k/ sound! Blink my eyes shut and turn my head down and toward the right. I push harder and finally utter the word, "kite," by jerking my jaw forward.

2. Now, when you have a good idea of what you do when you stutter, set up a program of change. Take all the elements—the excess baggage—that make up your stuttering pattern and consciously and deliberately attempt to *add* (exaggerate), *vary* (instead of jerking your head to the right, jerk it to the left) and

3

drop (stutter without that one mannerism) the separate aspects, one at a time. Start in an easy situation—alone, perhaps—and gradually increase the difficulty. Here is a chart that will help you organize your practice time:

head jerk	*Add*	*Vary*	*Drop*
	Monday, read aloud for 15 minutes.	Wednesday, read aloud for 15 minutes.	Friday, read aloud for 15 minutes.
	Exaggerate head jerk to the *left*.	*Exaggerate* easy head jerks to the *right*.	*Stop* use of head jerk.

(Follow this same plan for changing the other elements of your stuttering pattern; lip tensing, eye blink, etc.)

But, you say, I want to *stop* stuttering. Sure! But first you need to break up the habit pattern that you have built up over the years and this cannot be done instantly. The habit is powerful, because at the end of all the tension and struggle, the word does usually emerge. In a sense, then, stuttering works—so you persist in using the rituals that allow you to escape from stuttering. To break up a habit, you must alter its stereotyped nature.

> To break up a habit, you must alter its stereotyped nature.

3. When you are familiar with the various elements comprising your stuttering pattern and can alter them, then try to stutter more *easily* and *openly*. In a very real sense, the best advice I can give you is that you must learn to stutter better, with a minimum of tension and hurry. Instead of pushing so hard, try to ease out of your blocks by sliding into the first syllable of the word; start the *movement* and *sound* flow at the same time and glide into the word. Use strong movements of your lips and jaw and feel the shifts in those structures as you move *forward* through a word. Much of the agony and consequent social punishment of stuttering comes from tensing and holding back. Here are some instructions we gave to a stutterer recently who was learning to turn his stuttering on and off:

> When I raise my finger, you increase the pressure—
> to a real hard block. Then, as I lower my finger,
> slowly let the tension come out. That's right. Now, go

4

back and forth on your own: increase and decrease the tension. Learn to play with your blocks this way; get the *feel* of coming out of those hard fixations.

4. Now I am going to ask you to do a strange thing: *to stutter on purpose*. I know, it sounds weird but it works. Why? Because it helps to drain away the fear (what have you got to hide if you are willing to stutter on purpose?) and it provides a lot of experience practicing the act of stuttering in a highly voluntary and purposeful manner. The more you stutter on purpose, the less you hold back; and the less you hold back, the less you stutter. We once worked with a young exchange student who almost completely extinguished her stuttering in one week by doing negative practice. We were enmeshed in doctoral examinations so we gave her a hand-counter and told her: "There are 100,000 people living in Lansing; see how many you can talk to and show your stuttering." When I saw her seven days later she was haggard and worn but grinning broadly and not stuttering. Having taken us literally she had worked around the clock. Incredibly she had confronted 947 listeners! And she was totally unable to stutter involuntarily.

> "Stuttering on purpose...drains away the fear."

5. You must sharply reduce or eliminate the avoidances you use. Every time you substitute one word for another, use a sound or some trick to get speech started, postpone or give up an attempt at talking, you make it harder for yourself. Instead of diminishing when evaded, fears incubate and grow. The avoider must maintain constant vigilance and continually devise new ways to elude the dreaded words, listeners or situations. It's like pouring water into a leaking cask. Make a list of all your avoidances: What types do you use (starters, delaying tactics, etc.)? When, in what contexts do you use them? How frequently do you resort to evasion? In other words, prepare an avoidance inventory. Then, systematically vary and exaggerate each one; use the avoidances when you don't need to in a highly

> Make a list of all your avoidances:

voluntary manner. Finally, when you find yourself using an avoidance involuntarily, invoke a self-penalty; for example, if you avoid the word "chocolate," you must then use that word several times immediately thereafter. One of the best penalties is to explain to the listener the avoidance you have just used and why you should resist such evasions.

6. No stutterer is an island. Peoples' reactions to you and your interpretations of their reactions have, as you know, a profound effect upon your speech. You need to go out and renew your acquaintance with listeners; you need to talk to all kinds of people in all kinds of situations. Set up daily quotas or challenges for yourself; enter those tough speaking situations and demonstrate to yourself that you can, even though stuttering, get the message across. Any adventure is more fun when shared with congenial and helpful companions. Fortunately, there are self-help groups, with chapters in many parts of the country, that can provide information and support especially in this important aspect of altering old attitudes about your speech problem.*

7. Strange as it seems, you may find it difficult to adjust to more fluent speech. For years you have been laboring from block to block, you have been speaking a stuttering language. And, if you have used stuttering as an excuse or crutch, you may feel naked and exposed without it. The best antidote is to practice your new fluency until it becomes familiar to you. Plug your ears and read aloud, feeling the flow of words; shadow-talk along with speakers on radio or television; enroll for a speech course in your local area.

Licking the problem of stuttering, mastering your own mouth, takes time; it cannot be accomplished overnight. How long it will take you I cannot say, for no two stutterers approach the challenge in the same way or move at the same rate, but all have in common a beckoning mirage luring them ahead. Here then are the foundation blocks. Can you create from them stepping stones? Don't go any farther by freight. Express yourself!

*see Appendix A

Chapter 2

managing your stuttering
versus
your stuttering
managing you

Dorvan H. Breitenfeldt

Having been on a farm in Minnesota, I had the good fortune of attending a one room schoolhouse in which all eight grades were taught by one teacher. My stuttering began in the preschool years and continued to increase in severity. I compensated for my stuttering by becoming an academic over achiever. Because of my stuttering I quit school after completion of eighth grade and remained out of school for three years, during which time my stuttering increased greatly in severity. I did not use the telephone until I was seventeen, and my parents did my shopping for me. My speech consisted of long silent blocks. I frequently avoided talking altogether, or only said what I could without stuttering by using word substitution and circumlocution. I felt great shame and guilt, avoided outward stuttering at all costs, and often felt "why me?" Many times I cried alone about my stuttering, and even contemplated suicide because my stuttering had crept into all aspects of my life and brought it to a standstill. My stuttering was truly an "iceberg," with most of it beneath the surface.

7

Fortunately, I attended a six-week intensive group therapy program at the University of Minnesota at age seventeen. Unfortunately, I developed what is known as "lucky fluency" halfway through the session and returned home with essentially fluent speech, but with very little practice for **managing** my stuttering behaviors. At age seventeen I began my freshman year in high school where I remained fluent for about three months, after which time I experienced a sad relapse. I attended the same intensive therapy program one year later and fortunately returned home with the same amount of stuttering that I had before beginning the program. However, this time I obtained a great deal of experience in managing and controlling my stuttering, as well as the healthy attitude that I would likely be a lifetime stutterer and could not depend on fluency.

At the time of this writing, as I proceed into retirement from university teaching and administration, I find that my stuttering is still all there, in cycles, and can still be just as severe as it was prior to my first therapy. It looks as if chronic/advanced stuttering is truly "incurable" for most of us, therefore, we need to learn to live successful, fulfilling lives in spite of this constant companion.

> We need to learn to live successful, fulfilling lives in spite of this constant companion.

Since stuttering is only partially a communication problem, but more importantly a problem in human living, it must be attacked from all angles. We must work with the *person who stutters*, not just the stuttering. Due to the magnitude of the problem, my experience has been that the (chronic/confirmed) stutterer ideally needs intensive therapy to make changes rapidly and then be provided with the tools for an ongoing, and perhaps lifetime, maintenance program.

The three broad goals of a good therapeutic program are:

1. **Reduce Fear**: Strive to reduce word and situation fears, to change attitudes toward stuttering, and to objectively understand stuttering and build a good self image.

2. **Alter the stuttering pattern**: Study the stuttering symptoms. Let the stuttering out, develop an outward stuttering pattern, and learn techniques to manage the stuttering.

3. **Develop a maintenance program following therapy**... Stuttering, like so many human "illnesses/diseases/disorders/conditions" demands continuing self therapy and/or professional therapy.

The ideal treatment environment is frequently not available to many stutterers for various reasons. Some may be time restraints, availability of programs, finances, and perhaps the readiness of the stutterer to commit to participate on a full time basis. Nevertheless, there are many things the stutterer can do in self treatment or with limited professional help. By far the most important therapeutic principle is **advertising**, or acknowledging the fact that *you are a stutterer*. In every speaking situation, letting people know that you stutter creates a "stutter friendly" environment.

> There are many things the stutterer can do in self treatment or with limited professional help.

At first you may feel awkward admitting what you have tried so hard to hide, but after the dreaded "secret" is out, and you know that you don't have to worry so much about hiding your stuttering, you will begin to feel more at ease. Advertising is a lifetime technique and you should never attempt to pose as a fluent speaker. Honesty is always the best policy and is "cleansing for the soul."

Maintaining **eye contact** with your listener, especially during your stuttering blocks, is essential. Stutterers with poor eye contact show their feelings of embarrassment and negative reactions to their own stuttering.

> Good eye contact helps us become more effective speakers, and gives our listeners a better impression of us.

Eye contact is something the stutterer can work on without professional assistance. The best way to begin this practice is to maintain eye contact with yourself in front of a mirror while making phone calls and/or with someone else present. After the mirror sessions, then transfer the eye contact to all speaking situations. Good eye contact not only helps us become more effective speakers, but it also gives our listeners a better impression of us and our feelings toward our stuttering.

Before you can change your stuttering into more acceptable speech, you must first **identify and analyze** your particular stuttering symptoms. Two ways of accomplishing this are to observe your stuttering in the mirror and on video tape. Both the mirror work and the video must be done in the presence of others, as you will probably have very little stuttering, if any, when just talking to yourself.

Make a list of the specific things you do when you stutter. To do this you must give up the avoidance and postponement tricks you have been using to avoid your stuttering, and develop a nice, clean outward pattern of stuttering by going directly into your blocks. This will be the most difficult aspect of your self therapy, as most stutterers may never have exhibited *all* of their stuttering. Your outward stuttering will likely become much more severe; however, you know that it has always been that severe inwardly. To help you identify exactly when your stuttering blocks occur, which is absolutely necessary if you are going to change them, you need to use the **tallying technique**.

The steps in tallying are:
1. Go directly into the block without the use of starters, postponements, and other avoidance tricks
2. Stutter all the way through without retrial.
3. Stop immediately after the stuttered word.
4. Tally the block in a 3×5 memo book as: 1 2 3 4 5 6 7 8 9 10 etc.
5. Regain eye contact and continue until your next block, then mark (step 4.) in your tally book again, etc.

You should tally in all speaking situations, including talking on the telephone.

Word and situation fear reduction should be a part of every stuttering therapy program, since fears constitute a major portion of every stutterer's problems. The only known way to reduce fears is to confront them directly. Now you must deliberately go into your feared situations and go directly into all of your feared words. This will mean making many telephone calls, talking to many clerks in stores, stopping strangers and asking directions to various places, talking to groups and confronting all of your other feared situations. Always begin every speaking situation with "My name is ____. I am a stutterer and I am working to improve my speech." Maintain eye contact with your listener and tally all stuttering blocks. You will find that people are really very kind and helpful, as you have already established your "stutter friendly" environment by advertising your stuttering. In order to get your stuttering out in the open, tally your blocks effectively, develop good eye contact, and reduce your word and situation fears. You should expect to make at least 100 telephone calls and talk in 100 or more face to face speaking situations.

You are now ready to learn **Handling Techniques** to develop control of your stuttering so it no longer controls you. The handling technique which almost all stutterers find most effective is *prolongation*. Prolongation is starting the first sound of the word with a very light contact with your articulators (no tight lips, teeth, jaw or vocal cords) and prolonging or holding that first sound. Then say the rest of the word crisply and at a normal rate. Be sure not to prolong the second or other sounds in the word, unless you have a block on them. Do not slow down the overall rate of your speech, as it is highly unlikely that your stuttering has anything to do with talking too fast. Keep in mind that speech should always be easy and forward moving. Prolongation is a skill which will need a lot of practice. Prolonging on the first sound of every word, while first reading aloud to yourself and then to another person (so that you have real stuttering,) is an excellent way to practice. You will need to practice prolongation in many outside situations and on the telephone. Of course, the tallying is discontinued as soon as you begin to use your handling techniques. Another excellent handling technique is a *"pull-out,"* also known as an "in-block correction." When you are *"stuck in a block,"* you need to gain voluntary control during that block by intentionally releasing the tense structures, changing the tenseness to a light contact and moving forward through the rest of the word.

May I also encourage you to consider some **Lifestyle Changes** such as:

1. **Personal organization**. By structuring and organizing your daily routine, your cognitive abilities will be enhanced for more effective management of your stuttering.

2. **Outward appearance.** Develop an alert demeanor, friendly smile, and perhaps even make some changes in hair style and dress.

3. **Interpersonal and social relationships.** Develop an active social life to help you maintain control of your stuttering. Join groups such as Toastmasters or Toastmixers. Take a public speaking class. Humans are "pack animals," and it is important that the stutterer learn to "run with the pack."

4. **Personal health care.** Good physical fitness and a healthy diet improve the quality of life. We know that stutterers have a more difficult time managing their stuttering when they are not in good health.

5. **Take charge of your life.** This is paramount. You are a stutterer and it is your problem. Don't blame others. Plan to be a winner, not a loser.

Experience has demonstrated that stutterers who continue to manage their stuttering are those who also make major lifestyle changes.

The program summarized here sounds like an insurmountable task, but stuttering is a formidable opponent and the treatment must match, and even exceed, the size of the problem. You, who confront and conquer this adversary, have my greatest admiration and respect.

I wish you the very best as you continue through this venture called *life*.

Chapter **3**

stuttering: what you can do about it

Margaret Rainey

I deeply wish that I could reach every stutterer in the world to tell the story I am about to tell here. Last evening, as a speech clinician, I gave a speech to a large group of people who were vitally interested in stutterers and in the nature of stuttering. This morning as I sit drinking my coffee, and while the memories and experiences of last evening are vivid, I want to share my feelings and my knowledge with as many stutterers as possible.

It is interesting that I had no fear of that audience. I had no dread of the monsters of fear that once reared their ugly heads and choked off my words and even my thoughts. Yes, I am a stutterer, and I hope that it will help any stutterer who may read this to know that I was such a severe stutterer that I could not put two meaningful words together until I was twenty-four years old. Do I still stutter? Oh, I call myself a stutterer because I still have small interruptions in my speech now and then. But there's another more important reason why I call myself a stutterer. *I'm not trying to hide the fact anymore!* I learned long ago that the harder I tried to camouflage my stuttering, the more severely I stuttered. It was a vicious circle and I wanted out. So I got out!

> I learned long ago that the harder I tried to camouflage my stuttering, the more severely I stuttered.

How? I stopped stuttering severely with much less effort than I once used in trying in the wrong way to stop. And the wrong ways were to try to run from it, hide from it and forget it. I made the mistake of using every trick in the book to pretend to be a normal speaker, but none of the tricks worked for long. Failures only increased, and after years of agony I finally discovered that it was finally time to make an about-face. Why try to avoid and camouflage stuttering any longer? Who was I trying to fool? I knew that I stuttered, and so did my listeners. I finally took time out to ask myself why I should continue to fight the old, destructive feelings in the wrong way. I began to look at these feelings, and as I began to accept them and my stuttering, success in speaking began. It is interesting that the old ways of struggling were so difficult to give up. It felt as though I had an angry tiger by the tail and dared not let go.

I talked to the hearts of that excellent audience last evening and didn't pull any punches. Nobody should ever pull their punches when talking about the problem of stuttering. The problem is too vital to be treated in any other manner than with the truth. After the session was over I was gathering my notes together when I looked up and in front of me stood a young man in the throes of trying to say something. We shook hands and I listened and waited. A severe stutterer he was—so severe that apparently he dared not introduce himself. We sat down so that we might be as comfortable as possible, and in his unique pattern of speech, he asked some pertinent questions about himself and his stuttering.

The young man's first question had to do with whether there might be a physical cause for his stuttering. He explained that he was five years old when he was hit by a car and said that the scar was still on his neck. He wondered what other reason there could be to prevent him from saying his words fluently. To be struck by a car is a traumatic incident indeed, but I told this young man that his real scars were psychological ones and that the physical one on his neck was only skin deep. He was anxious to know what those psychological scars were and I was anxious to tell him that *he* knew better than *I*. "The answers lie in your looking closely at your stuttering pattern and at yourself."

This sincere young man asked a gut level question which all stutterers ask, "What do people think of me?" He said that he was weary of laughter and ridicule. I tried to explain that to a great extent he was putting the cart before the horse, the most important question that he should investigate is *what he thinks of himself.* I strongly suggested that he was by far his worst critic and that he had been living for years being his worst critic. But I also told him that he had lived most of his verbal life upon the judgments and misjudgments of others.

> He was by far his worst critic.

"It's your job," I emphasized, "to help other people understand. There's nothing like understanding that makes for the acceptance of differences. Help normal speakers to understand that what they are doing to stutterers is well-meaning, but wrong." I explained to him that we both knew that stuttering is indeed behavior which is different and that realistically we should not expect a person who has never had the problem to know what to do about it when he sees and hears it in another person.

I went further with this explanation because he was listening so intently. "When your listener looks away from you, it is because he thinks that you *want* him to look away. Ask him not to do it. It's as simple as this! When a listener laughs out of embarrassment, it might be

> When your listener looks away from you, it is because he thinks that you *want* him to look away.

tremendously helpful to realize that the embarrassment is the listener's, not yours. Don't borrow trouble, you've got enough of your own!"

We both agreed that the stutterer's listener should react to him just as though he is a normal person with an interesting kind of speech difference. That's how stutterers *want* to be treated, but they never request it. As a matter of fact, I had to tell him that *I* would feel more comfortable if he would look at me while we talked, and it was interesting that as he began to look at me he struggled less and less.

Now it was my turn to ask a question and I asked whether or not he thought that he had suffered long enough in feeling himself to be inferior. I indicated that his world of agony did not hinge solely upon his stumbling speech. His attitudes about himself, his listener and his speech were important. Hadn't he struggled long enough, and in vain, to pretend as best he could that he was not a stutterer? Be done with swinging at these straw men! They were *his* ghosts, not his listeners. I told him that his fear of stuttering is the greater part of the reason that he stutters. He seemed to understand.

It was my turn to ask still another question. "When was the last time you discussed your stuttering with anyone?" He said that he had never talked about it with anyone. "You know," I replied, "just as eye communication during speech is one of the most important ways to tell the other person that you have something to communicate, so is open discussion of your stuttering and your feelings about it." One of the biggest mistakes that stutterers and normal speakers make is to consider this problem to be a verboten, hush-hush subject.

I explained to this handsome young man (who had described himself as being repulsive) that no two stutterers stutter alike. Yet, every stutterer possesses two very strong and incapacitating feelings in common: *Fear* and *Anxiety*. Herein lies the heart of his problem. If the fear of stuttering can be reduced, then certainly stuttering itself can be reduced.

He wanted to know whether or not there would ever really be a cure for him. All stutterers search for the magic pill. I told him that a "cure" is rare, but not impossible. "But this doesn't mean that you have to live the rest of your verbal life in struggling. Why wrestle with those words so hard? You're even struggling between words," I pointed out to him. "You must be very tired!" He agreed that he was. Then I told him something else that gave him pause: "Don't make the mistake of trying to compete with others. Compete with yourself—from day to day, from speaking situation to speaking situation and from word to word. Competing with yourself means that you learn to understand *and cope with* the fears that surround your speech.

The young man told me that he knew of no place to go for help and some relief from his stuttering. I answered that it would be ideal if he could find some place and named a few university clinics where highly qualified speech clinicians with deep and intuitive understanding, work with stutterers. But I also emphasized to him that he could become his own speech clinician. He didn't get this idea right away, so I gave him some concrete suggestions.

"When a problem exists," I explained, "the first thing to do is to examine it carefully with the hope of discovering what is wrong." I told him that one of the most constructive things that he could do for himself was to observe himself several times a day in a mirror as he talked. Although it is a tough row to hoe at first, there is nothing as therapeutic as self confrontation. "Be as objective as possible," I found myself almost pleading with him. "Look and listen closely and discover just what it is that you are doing when you stutter. And after you make these discoveries, *refuse* to make them again. Easier said than done? Yup! But it's well worth every effort that you put into it. When you begin to really accept yourself as the stutterer you are, you're on your way to much easier speech and most certainly to greater peace of mind." I also suggested that he get himself a tape recorder and listen to himself with long ears. He'd soon discover that 90% of his stuttering consists of behavior that has made his stuttering more severe, not less severe.

The job is to think and work in a positive manner. The job involves coming to realize that those head jerks, eye blinks, tongue clicks, postponements on feared words, substituting non-feared words for feared ones, and the thousand and one ways in learning "how not to stutter" are not helping to get those words out. They are preventing the words from being said strongly, aggressively and fluently.

"Those blocks may look and sound like monsters to you now, but you can turn them into straw men. Attack them! You must *refuse* to allow your words and fears to control you. Remember that one failure leads to another, and you're really trapped if you're caught in the web of misunderstanding the dynamics of your stuttering symptoms." He was listening intently.

Know and remember that success begets success

"Know and remember that success begets success and self pity will get you nowhere!" Yes, he was still listening intently and was seeming to absorb the messages. Does working on yourself take guts? You bet it does! Does using your guts pay off? You bet it does!

My parting words to this young stutterer, in whom I hoped a wise investment had been made, were "Try it! You'll like it!...and let me hear from you."

And now, five cups of coffee later, I hope again that I have touched and helped another stutterer to help himself.

Chapter 4

two sides of the coin

Hugo H. Gregory

I grew up as a youngster with a developing problem of stuttering. Then at ages 14 to 16, I had therapy during two six-week summer programs. When I was a junior in college, I became a student in the field of speech-language pathology, followed by my professional career. I want to share with you some of most important things I have learned about stuttering therapy using my own experiences during these periods as a frame of reference.

Like the many teenagers and adults I have known during my professional career, my goal in therapy was to stop stuttering and speak fluently. This was a very natural desire, considering the frustration and embarrassment associated with the problem. I perceived treatment as consisting of being silent (no conversation) for periods of time in which syllables, words, and sentences were practiced as I learned ways to control and eliminate stuttering.

I had not thought about people having normal disfluencies in their speech. In what was called "word analysis" we learned a rule for the production of each consonant, and as we said a word we thought of the rule for the initial consonant. For example, the rule for 'b,' a voiced consonant, was "start the voice from below the tongue (in the voice box) and make a smooth movement into the following vowel"; for 'p' a voiceless consonant, "start the voice from above the tongue, etc." In word analysis, transitions between sounds were very smooth, but words were spoken one at a time. I wrote home that I was unlearning the old habits of stuttering and learning a new way of talking. At the end of two weeks, we were allowed to converse using word analysis. To a girl, with whom I had been writing notes while on silence, I was now able to say, "P-A-T, W-O-U-L-D Y-O-U L-I-K-E T-O G-O T-O T-H-E M-O-V-I-E-S S-A-T-U-R-D-A-Y N-I-G-H-T?" After that first weekend, we were not allowed to converse again for almost two weeks. I wrote more notes to Pat and practiced phrasing from a manual of sentences. In phrasing, only the first word of the phrase was analyzed. I was able to say, "Pat / would you like to go / to the Biltmore Hotel / for dinner / on Saturday night?" In addition to the improvement in speech, I progressed in two weeks from a movie to dinner at a fancy hotel. This was very exciting for a 15-year-old!

This was my first introduction to what we now designate as the "speak-more-fluently" approach to therapy. Little or no attention was given to monitoring the way in which my speech was disrupted by blocking voice flow at the vocal folds or closing my lips tightly and pushing hard when attempting words beginning with "P" or "B." The emphasis was on replacing stuttering with word analysis and phrasing.

Although I was conscientious in practicing words and sentences every day using my rules, and being more open to others about work on my speech, several months after I returned home I began to have increasingly more trouble. However, like most people who stutter that I have known, every therapy method is helpful to some extent, and this was true for me. I never had as much difficulty again as I had before that first summer.

A year later when I went back to review methods of word analysis and phrasing, I began to realize that I had concentrated on the speech aspect of therapy and missed a great deal of the part having to do with attitude. I recalled that the clinicians had talked about how people who stutter become very sensitive about the fluency of their speech. I began to see that if I stuttered I was very hard on myself!

Later in college, Wendell Johnson's ideas helped me to understand that I should not attempt to evaluate myself as "either I am a stutterer or I am not a stutterer." I began to view myself more and more as a person who stuttered sometimes as he talked. I realized that I was going through a process of change. I also saw more clearly that I had to take responsibility for making others feel comfortable in my presence. Since I was doing something constructive, I could smile more about my difficulties. When I was more at ease, I stuttered less and felt that those around me were more comfortable. During my second year in college, the writings of Charles Van Riper influenced me to be willing to stutter on purpose. Keeping good eye contact with my listener as I introduced myself, I was able to say, "I'm Hugo Gre-Greeegory," varying the way in which I feigned stuttering. I was amazed by the effects of this. I realized that I could not fear stuttering as much if I was willing to do it on purpose! Within a short time my expectation of difficulty introducing myself began to decrease more and more. I employed voluntary stuttering in many situations. These beginning insights into

> I realized that I could not fear stuttering as much if I was willing to do it on purpose!

the attitudinal features of stuttering therapy have been expanded as I have helped other people who stutter to understand how their therapy is a step by step process involving **both** attitude **and** speech change.

When I went to Northwestern University to study "speech correction," as the field of speech-language pathology was known at that time, I realized that some of the reading I had done and some of my own experiences, such as the use of voluntary stuttering, had prepared me to understand another model of therapy known as the "stutter-more-fluently" approach. The objective of this method was to reduce the tendencies to inhibit and avoid disfluency and stuttering by monitoring, analyzing, and modifying stuttering: i.e., learning to stutter more easily but not stop it! In my own continuing self-therapy, I began to study my stuttering more and learned to modify instances of stuttering, first by immediately going back to say a word in a different, more relaxed way, and then by modifying the stuttering by easing the tension and moving forward more smoothly and easily.

At this point, therapy based on both "speak-more-fluently" and "stutter-more-fluently" approaches had helped. I was able to use relaxed initiations with phrasing. I was willing to modify my speech just after an instance of stuttering or even during an occurrence of stuttering. Just as I have now seen in many people during therapy, my self-confidence about talking was continuing to increase as I explored and changed not only my stuttering, but also my speech in general!

As I progressed in my professional life, I began to recognize inadequacies of a therapy program based on either an avoidance reduction/stuttering modification approach or a direct fluency enhancing model. The stutter-more-easily approach may not result in post-therapy speech that is as normally fluent as it could be. On the other hand, building fluency may not reduce the fear of stuttering as much as is desirable. I began to combine the two methods in my work with others, in ways similar to what I had done in my own therapy. I have guided teenagers and adults who stutter toward monitoring their stuttering by changing and modifying it. The person learns to stutter more easily, followed by the monitoring of relaxed speech beginnings, smooth transitions between words, more adequate pause time between phrases, and resistance of time pressure. In my clinical practice and teaching I called this **working with two sides of the coin:** decreasing sensitivity to stuttering and disfluency in general is one side of the coin, and then building fluency is the other side of the coin. I adopted a gesture, pointing to the palm of my hand as decreasing sensitivity to stuttering and the back of my hand as building fluency, emphasizing an attitude of doing both continuously, as I turned my hand first one way and then the other!

Decreasing sensitivity to stuttering is one side of the coin, and building fluency is the other side.

With reference to this personal and professional experiences, I help clients to do the following:

- **Listen and watch** their own stuttering (using audio and video recordings), gradually seeing that they can reduce the tension involved, thus being able to stutter with "full tension" or "50% reduction of tension." Clients need considerable support for this negative practice that is only done during therapy sessions, in practice alone at home, or with a person with whom they feel comfortable. Concealment has been a strong motivation since childhood. Almost immediately, most express a feeling of relief that comes with, as Dr. Van Riper would have said, "touching their stuttering."

- Based on observations of each individual's stuttering, I then help a person to **reduce tension** and make a more adaptive, easy, relaxed approach to a phrase, with a smoother movement between sounds and words; then pausing at the end of a phrase and repeating the process. In the parlance of stuttering therapy, this has become known as ERA-SM (easy relaxed approach-smooth movement). An important objective is to contrast the tension and fragmentation of negative practice with ERA-SM and for the persons who stutter to monitor what they are doing.

- To **resist time pressure** in communication, which is a problem for everyone, but even more so for people who stutter that have insecurities about initiating and maintaining fluent speech, I teach delayed response. Now that clients have more confidence in initiating speech, they can learn to delay, using a count of two in their minds as a guide, before speaking in situations such as when answering a question, giving their phone number, taking their turn in conversations or even between phrases as they talk.

- Clients also learn to use *"voluntary disfluency"* by adding normal disfluencies in their speech, such as "I, I, I," "have you, have you," "It's uh, uh, uh, plane, it's uh uh superman." As the person gets good at the voluntary disfluency, I challenge them to add more of "a real stutter" in their speech. Obviously, this helps to douse the fear of disfluency and stuttering. Many people who stutter have not thought about all speakers as being disfluent.

- All during treatment, I stress that therapy activities not only help to reduce stuttering, but also enable a person to "**be a better than average speaker**," even though there may occasional stuttering. In this connection, the last objective is to build flexibility in speaking by varying the length of phrases, speech rate, loudness and inflection, etc. ERA-SM undergoes change as therapy continues, becoming speech that is just more relaxed. Monitoring speech should not be seen as a chore, but as an opportunity to learn the many things people can do with their speech mechanisms. Self-monitoring is involved in all skilled behavior! Better speakers are able to keep in mind how they are talking, as well as what they are saying. However, as new responses are acquired, less attention is required.

All of these procedures for modifying speech are done first in easier speaking situations and gradually in ones that are more difficult. Lastly, since each individual's stuttering problem is different, each person must become a problem solver focusing on certain feelings, beliefs, and experiences. People who stutter should see how effective change involves evaluating what they do in situations, planning for the next time, and continuing the process of self-evaluation and change.

what you can do to help yourself

Lois A. Nelson

If only you could talk without stuttering! You may be frustrated when stuttering occurs. You may get discouraged and angry with yourself and at the world. Nothing you try seems to be effective for long. At its mildest, stuttering can be annoying. At its worst, it interferes greatly with communication and with your life. Past experiences may have strengthened the belief that nothing you do will make any difference in how you talk. That's where you're wrong.

It is possible to change the behavior that you do when you stutter. Not by magic. Not by asking others to do the changing for you. The ingredients of change are firmly rooted in knowledge. You need information about the **process of speaking fluently**. You need information about the **disorder of stuttering**. And, you need to experiment with **various ways of stuttering**. A tall order but not if you have a plan.

To begin with, change your focus. One of the most difficult concepts to grasp is this: the behavior that occurs when you *try-not-to-stutter* contributes to the severity of the stuttering. Try the opposite behavior: *try to stutter*. Become very familiar with exactly what you do while stuttering if you are to change it. Too difficult? You simply want the stuttering to go away — never to occur again. That's a normal reaction. You dislike repeating. You do not want to hear or see or physically feel stuttering. The experiences of feeling "stuck" are frustrating and perhaps frightening. Tremors in your lips or jaw may give rise to panic. It is hard work. Harder than you have ever done before. It is less fearful to study and analyze stuttering under the guidance of a fluency therapist. But you can do some of the identifying and categorizing of behavior on your own if you remember to do this "change work" in small doses. Don't overwhelm yourself. Tomorrow is another day. It took years for stuttering to develop to the level and in the particular pattern that occurs at this point in time. The process of unraveling the pattern and changing the disfluent behavior takes time also.

First, **study how fluent talking is done**. You need to understand the way in which the activity of talking occurs physically. Sometimes explanations are inaccurate because information is omitted in the writer's attempt to simplify and to be brief. Obtain a textbook from the library. Search out information that provides an explanation of how breathing for living and breathing for speaking occur and differ. Sit quietly. Focus on breathing in a natural way. Discover how *air* flows in and out of your mouth. When you begin to speak, part of the process changes. Discover how *voice* starts easily and gently when you are relaxed and unhurried. Notice how your lips and tongue and lower jaw *move* to shape the air and voice into words. Feel that you can *move smoothly* through a word and move from one word to another without stopping. That's fluency, or at least part of it. Think about the number of words you can speak comfortably in a sentence without straining for air. Focus on the speed of talking. Some words in a sentence are said quickly; others are said more slowly to make the message meaningful. The pitch of your voice rises when asking a question and loudness increases when angry. When you talk fluently, many physical actions

Don't just enjoy fluency when it occurs. Learn from it.

occur in a coordinated, sequenced fashion. That's one of the keys. Study these actions. *Fluent talking* is the behavior that you are trying to do more of. You need a solid awareness of the fluency model. Observe others when they talk fluently as well as observe yourself. Take notes. Don't just enjoy fluency when it occurs. Learn from it. What does fluent talking sound like, look like, physically feel like in your body? What does it emotionally feel like in your mind?

Second, **study behavior**. Select a book on the introduction to psychology. Read the chapters that discuss stimuli and responses and how they are chained together. Learn how behavior can be strengthened or weakened, or counter-conditioned. Stuttering behavior is complex to be sure, but it behaves in lawful or expected ways just as other behaviors do. It is less difficult to shape stuttering than you may think. Stuttering is predictable. It can be altered through applying information from your study of behavior. Incorporate that knowledge into the therapy plan you design.

Third, **become informed about the nature of stuttering**. Much has been written which can reduce the mystery for you. Experts have described the speech characteristics of stuttering (the repetitions, prolongations, or stopping of air flow, voice or movement); the accompanying behavior (such as jaw jerks, eye blinks, saying um or well); the typical feelings and attitudes; how stuttering develops over time; what is known about causes, and so on. The depth of knowledge is your choice. Be guided by your interest level and by a desire to become as objective and unemotional as possible about the disorder.

...become as objective and unemotional as possible about the disorder.

Fourth, **develop accuracy in analyzing the stuttering in detail**. Analysis is not a task of counting stuttering moments. Instead, determine which kinds of stuttering behavior you do such as repetitions, prolongations or stopping air flow, voice or movement. Do several types of behavior occur in a sequence? Is there a pattern? Keep notes. To observe merely that you repeat, for example, is not sufficiently descriptive to be helpful to you later. Ask yourself what size unit is repeated: a sound? a syllable? a word? How many times is a syllable repeated when stuttering mildly? When stuttering severely? Where within the word does the repeated portion occur: at the beginning? Further within the word? At a fast rate? Is the repeated portion done with effort? Examine each type of stuttering behavior that you do in similar detail

Fifth, **develop ability to cope with the stuttering moment itself**. Build on your analysis skills. Direct yourself to focus on the stuttering as it is occurring in the *present* time-frame. Reliving *past* difficulty or anticipating *future* failure is unhelpful in this section of the "change work." The residue from these negative emotions provides few clues for coping effectively with stuttering as it is happening *now*. As you learn to listen, to view, and to physically feel the stuttering, continue to ask: "What occurred right there?" And "What did I do next?" and "Then what resulted?" Hunt for the consequences of your actions. Make notes on your findings.

Experiment with stuttering. Choose a word. Next, say that word while holding your breath. Hopefully, you will find that it's impossible. But you can change that act of "breath holding" just as you will be able to change other stuttering behaviors. How? Think back to the way in which the word is said smoothly. *Focus on the feeling of movement*. Get a clear picture of that smoothly said word. You can change consistently if you know clearly what you **are doing** and what you **are trying to do**.

Will this practice in "breath holding" or any other stuttering done purposely get out-of-control? Temporarily it may. Here's how to cope. Practice doing milder types of stuttering. You can end the breath holding immediately by "letting go" of it. Don't finish the word. Just stop. Get calmer. Try again, later or the next day. Stay in contact with stuttering as much as you can in small doses. Experiment similarly with the other types of stuttering behavior that you do.

Sixth, **understand emotions**. Check out the psychology book again. Look for sections which discuss emotions and their impact on performance and learning. *Fear and embarrassment* — two common negative emotions — are known to interfere with ability to **focus on** and to **perform** an activity. This holds true for speaking just as much as for sports. What's the issue? Do such emotions prevent your entering fully into situations? The information you derive from those speaking experiences will be inaccurate and mislead you. In turn, you make errors in problem solving and the desired changes in your speech do not occur.

Devise a therapy plan to include practice in desensitizing yourself to disruptive emotion and to stuttering. You won't totally eliminate reactions to events that trigger stress for you, but you can learn to reduce the level of stress until communication is more manageable. It is difficult to attempt speaking and to practice strategies once stuttering and fear seem to be out-of-control. Most persons who stutter need the direction and support of a fluency therapist during this aspect of the "change work."

Seventh, **become an effective problem solver**. It's not a complicated procedure. Locate a book at the library that explains the steps of "how to problem-solve" and work to develop skills in using that format. Apply this format to the changes you want to make in the stuttering behavior. Problem solving is a logical and objective way to examine issues and to generate solutions. Random trial-and-error wastes your time and energy. It is not productive.

Eighth, **consider the possibility that you may have two fluency problems: stuttering and cluttering**. Over half of those who stutter have both of them. Does it really matter? Absolutely. Your therapy program should be revised to include strategies for both aspects if they exist. Otherwise, stuttering improves very little.

Here's one clue: In stuttering you know what you want to say but can't get the word started. Does your stuttering occur in response to talking too fast, having difficulty finding words or difficulty organizing your thoughts? Do many ideas flood your mind quickly, but then you lose them before the idea is stated? Determining whether you clutter in addition to stutter is not easy for a teen or adult. The cluttering may be masked by severe stuttering and struggle behavior. Expect the combination of problems that occur in cluttering to vary and to range in severity just as occurs with stuttering.

Here's a coping strategy for cluttering: Slow your rate to give yourself more time to organize thoughts and retrieve words. Then you will be attending to the message of speaking as well as the mechanics.

Is that all? Of course not. It is a bare-bones structure upon which to build. It is the minimum in information and experiences which may enable you to make changes in your speech and emotions. Think positively. There is much you can do to make changes in the way you talk, and how you think about your talking,

The results are worth the time and effort you put into the task.

Good luck in your quest for achieving your goals.

Chapter 6

message to a stutterer

Joseph G. Sheehan

If your experience as a stutterer is anything like mine, you've spent a good part of your life listening to suggestions, such as "relax, think what you have to say, have confidence, take a deep breath," or even to "talk with pebbles in your mouth." And by now, you've found that these things don't help; if anything, they make you worse.

There's a good reason why these legendary remedies fail, because they all mean suppressing your stuttering, covering up, doing something artificial. And the more you cover up and try to avoid stuttering, the more you will stutter.

Your stuttering is like an iceberg. The part above the surface, what people see and hear, is really the smaller part. By far the larger part is the part underneath—the shame, the fear, the guilt, all those other feelings that come to us when we try to speak a simple sentence and can't.

Like me, you've probably tried to keep as much of that iceberg

Your stuttering is like an iceberg.

under the surface as possible. You've tried to cover up, to keep up a pretense as a fluent speaker, despite long blocks and pauses too painful for either you or your listener to ignore. You get tired of this phony role. Even when your crutches work you don't feel very good about them. And when your tricks fail you feel even worse. Even so, you probably don't realize how much your coverup and avoidance keep you in the vicious circle of stuttering.

In psychological and speech laboratories we've uncovered evidence that stuttering is a conflict, a special kind of conflict between going forward and holding back—an "approach-avoidance" conflict. You want to express yourself but are torn by a competing urge to hold back, because of fear. For you as for other stutterers, this fear has many sources and levels. The most immediate and pressing fear is of stuttering itself and is probably secondary to whatever caused you to stutter in the first place.

Your fear of stuttering is based largely on your shame and hatred of it. The fear is also based on playing the phony role, pretending your stuttering doesn't exist. You can do something about this fear, if you have the courage. You can be open about your stuttering, above the surface. You can learn to go ahead and speak anyway, to go forward in the face of fear. In short, you can be yourself. Then you'll lose the insecurity that always comes from posing. You'll reduce that part of the iceberg beneath the surface. And this is the part that has to go first. Just being yourself, being open about your stuttering, will give you a lot of relief from tension.

Here are two principles which you can use to your advantage, once you understand them: they are (1) your stuttering doesn't hurt you; (2) your fluency doesn't do you any good. There's nothing to be ashamed of when you stutter and there's nothing to be proud of when you are fluent.

Most stutterers wince with each block, experiencing it as a failure, a defect. For this reason they struggle hard not to stutter and therefore stutter all the more. They get themselves into a vicious circle which can be diagrammed as follows:

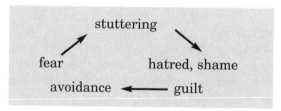

Stuttering is a lonesome kind of experience. Possibly you haven't seen too many stutterers and those you have seen you have avoided like the plague. Just as there may be people who know you or have seen you or even heard you who don't realize that there's anything wrong with your speech, so those who have a speech handicap similar to yours keep it concealed. For this reason few realize that almost one percent of the population stutter, that there are more than three million stutterers in the United States today. That many famous people from history have had essentially the same problem, including Moses, Demosthenes, Charles Lamb, Charles Darwin, and Charles I of England. More recently, George VI of England, Somerset Maugham, Marilyn Monroe, and the T. V. personalities, Garry Moore and Jack Paar have been stutterers at some time in their lives. In your speech problem you may not be as unique or as much alone as you had thought!

Each adult stutterer has his individual style made up usually of tricks or crutches which are conditioned to the fear and have become automatic. Yet they all suffer from basically the same disorder, whether they choose to call it stammering, a speech impediment, or something else. *How* you stutter is terribly important. You don't have a choice as to whether you stutter, but you do have a choice as to how you stutter. Many stutterers have learned as I have learned, that it is possible to stutter easily and with little struggle and tension. The most important key

...you do have a choice as to how you stutter.

in learning how to do this is openness: getting more of the iceberg above the surface, being yourself, not struggling and fighting against each block and looking your listener calmly in the eye, never giving up in a speech attempt once started, never avoiding words or ducking out of situations, taking the initiative in speaking even when doing a lot of stuttering. All these are fundamental in any successful recovery from stuttering.

You can stutter your way out of this problem. As long as you greet each stuttering block with shame and hatred and guilt, you will feel fear and avoidance toward speaking. This fear and avoidance and guilt will lead to still more stuttering, and so on. Most older therapies failed to break up the vicious triangle because they sought to prevent or eliminate the occurrence of stuttering which is the result of the fear. You can do better by reducing your shame and guilt and hatred of stuttering which are the immediate causes of the fear. Because stuttering can be maintained in this vicious triangle basis, there are many adults who could help themselves to speak with much less struggle if they would accept their stuttering, remain open about it, and do what they could to decrease their hatred of it.

Some individuals, given a start in the right direction, can make substantial headway by themselves. Others need more extensive and formal speech therapy.

Because you stutter, it doesn't mean you are any more maladjusted than the next person. Systematic evaluation of objective research using modern methods of personality study show no typical personality pattern for stutterers, and no consistent differences between those who stutter and those who don't. Maybe a little fortification with that knowledge will help you to accept yourself as a stutterer and feel more comfortable and be open about it.

If you are like most of the 3 million stutterers in this country, clinical treatment will not be available to you. Whatever you do you'll have to do pretty much on your own with what ideas and sources you can use. It isn't a question of whether self-treatment is desirable. Clinic treatment in most instances will enable you to make more systematic progress. This is particularly true if you are among those stutterers who, along with people who don't stutter, have personality and emotional problems. Every stutterer does try to treat his own case in a sense anyway. He has to have a modus operandi, a way of handling things, a way of going about the task of talking.

I have tried to set down some basic ideas which are sounder and more workable than the notions that most stutterers are given about their problem.

You might go about it this way. Next time you go into a store or answer the telephone, see how much you can go ahead in the face of fear. See if you can accept the stuttering blocks you will have more calmly so that your listener can do the same, and in all other situations see if you can begin to accept openly the role of someone who will for a time stutter and have fears and blocks in his speech. But show everyone that you don't intend to let your stuttering keep you from taking part in life. Express yourself in every way possible and practical. Don't let your stuttering get between you and the other person. See if you can get to the point where you have as little urge for avoidance and concealment in important situations as you would when you speak alone. And when you do stutter—and you will—be matter of fact about it. Don't waste

> Express yourself in every way possible and practical.

your time and frustrate yourself by trying to speak with perfect fluency. If you've come into adult life as a stutterer, the chances are that you'll always be a stutterer, in a sense. But you don't have to be the kind of stutterer that you are—you can be a mild one without much handicap.

Age is not too important a factor, but emotional maturity is. One of our most successful recoveries on record is that of a 78-year-old retired bandmaster who resolved that before he died he would conquer his handicap. He did.

In summary, see how much of that iceberg you can bring up above the surface. When you get to the point where you're concealing nothing from your listener, you won't have much handicap left. You can stutter your way out of this problem, if you do it courageously and openly.

toward freer speech

Frederick P. Murray

Before embarking on the path of endeavoring to improve your speech, I suggest that you do some preliminary work along the lines of constructive and positive thinking. Motivation directed toward the goal of better speech is of the utmost importance if you are to move successfully along the road to better fluency. I would encourage you to tap whatever sources you have within you or might attain from religion, friends, or books, and utilize them toward this aim. Belief in yourself and cooperation with others are vital necessities as you undertake your task.

Do not expect the solution to years of confirmed stuttering to be rapid. Many stut-

> Belief in yourself and cooperation with others are vital necessities...

terers have mistakenly believed that if only the "cause" could be found, a fast cure would result. Will the fire that is consuming a house extinguish itself merely because the match that started it has been discovered in an adjacent field? Stuttering in its advanced stages is self-perpetuating, much like a fire. It feeds on itself; fears of words and speaking situations act as cues to intensify it. Clearly, there will be a need for you to face up to, confront, and work upon your problem. This will call for active efforts on your part because strongly conditioned motor responses are changed by *action*, not by thought.

Many of you have heard about the wonders of hypnosis and may look to this technique to provide a quick answer. Rest assured that this has been tried throughout the years, but almost invariably with only temporary and fleeting success. It does not serve to build up the

> Strongly conditioned motor responses are changed by *action*, not by thought.

necessary resistance to the innumerable threats that now haunt you with regard to your oral communication. The ability to cope with these factors will come about only gradually as you change both your speaking behavior and personal attitudes, and as you adjust yourself to the new self-role that improved speech will thrust upon you. It is similar to an enormously fat man attempting to lose a hundred pounds. To do this safely he must do so at a rate that his heart and body can tolerate. If it occurs too rapidly, deep wrinkles will appear, and in extreme cases, he may collapse from the rapid change that his organism has undergone. The body needs a chance to integrate itself to each successive level of improvement in weight reduction. So it is with the stutterer who must adjust himself to better fluency. Therefore, I urge you to have tolerance with yourself as you proceed along the way. Do not demand the impossible at first! There is no law that states you must pick up the heavy end of the log every time.

Judging from my personal acquaintance with dozens of stutterers who have achieved a good recovery, I note there is not one who would claim to be completely fluent at all times. In other words, each one admits to occasional moments of disfluent speech and residuals of stuttering. However, persons who have not stuttered say that their speech fits approximately the same description. Some stutterers have arrived at a point where their overall speaking skill surpasses that possessed by the average speaker. So keep your head high!

Your ultimate goal, no matter how it may be reached, is to convince yourself that you are capable of speaking in oral communication situations. This is the opposite of saying to yourself that you cannot succeed in these situations because you cannot talk. The important thing, however, is that the conviction is thorough enough that it reflects itself automatically via your emotions and feelings. Remember, our speech is a mirror of how we feel at any given moment in time, and feelings can be changed.

To help you in your goal the following guidelines are offered to provide information that should assist you.

Perhaps the first concrete step you should take is to acquaint yourself with your stuttering behavior. Odd as this may seem, few severe stutterers know what they are doing that interferes with the forward flow of speech. In order to carry this out effectively, you must first learn to keep in touch with yourself during your moments of stuttering. This is in direct contrast to attempting to run away from yourself and doing everything possible to try to avoid the occurrence of stuttering. Feedback of various types will assist you in this self-study endeavor. For example, you can look at yourself in a mirror and assess what you are doing while you make a phone call likely to elicit stuttering. Is it possible to record your speech in a communicatively stressful situation, then play the tape back for the purpose of careful analysis? Painful as this may seem, it is one good way to bring yourself to grips with your problem. If you can achieve a sufficient number of these behavior-exploring experiences you will discover that your stuttering is not a constant and fixed behavior; rather, it is something that varies greatly and is composed of some parts that are not handicapping. Regardless of the severity of the longer, highly abnormal blockages, each and every stutterer has some degree of easy moments of stuttering in his speech. These miniature stutterings represent goals in themselves. If you can learn to whittle the others down to similar proportion, more of your scoreable difficulty will have disappeared. This leads to the realization that there are countless ways in which to stutter. Even though you may have no choice as to whether or not you will stutter, you do have the choice of *how you stutter*.

> Few severe stutterers know what they are doing that interferes with the forward flow of speech.

> You do have the choice of *how you stutter*.

It is also necessary to develop an awareness of the feelings you have in connection with your stuttering. Often your speech difficulty may seem to overwhelm you so much that you are unable to evaluate objectively the emotions that are intimately tied with it. Anxiety, guilt and shame are usually linked to severe speech blockages. Clearly, there will be a need to make some degree of separation between these compulsive forces. Success in accomplishing this should deprive the stuttering of some of its most powerful maintaining factors. Your fundamental task is twofold: alter your speech behavior, and bring about positive changes in your self-perceptions and feelings. A longstanding psychological principle states that one way to influence emotions and bring about a change in feeling is to deal directly with the outward behaviors that are associated with, and are the chief symptoms of, these inner states. If you can modify the severity of your more grotesque speech interruptions by substituting more relaxed forward-flowing speech movements, you will be putting this psychological principle into action. One excellent way to encourage this is by carefully planning certain speaking experiences. Your immediate goal should be to allow yourself to *stutter openly* and without tension and struggle. Do not try to speak as fluently as possible! By deliberately permitting yourself to prolong the initial sounds of many of the words you use, you will be taking the psychological offensive. You will be providing yourself with new outlets through which much of the built-up anticipatory fear can be dissipated, rather than steadily mounting up inside you. In addition, you will be giving your neurophysiological system an opportunity to work in better harmony rather than having one component counteract another. You will be confronting rather than avoiding your problem; the habitual avoidance of speech situations and feared words will get you *nowhere* in the long run. The sooner you are able to give up your holding-back behavior, the better! The following guidelines can serve to help you along the path of recovery from stuttering:

1. The handicap of stuttering consists mostly of learned behaviors. These can be unlearned.

2. Stuttering behaviors can be changed. Remember, you can choose how to stutter even if you cannot choose not to stutter.

3. A person can stutter in many ways.

4. Emotions can be altered by modifying symptoms associated with them.

5. Fear and avoidance lessen as confrontation is increased.

6. Long lasting improvement is unlikely to occur in a scientific laboratory setting. Learn to assemble your own portable laboratory and use it in the real world.

7. Accept the self-identity role of "stutterer" to whatever extent you may need it to help lessen negative emotions tied in with stuttering. As your stuttering diminishes, you can adjust this role to be more and more that of an effective communicator.

8. Recovery is probably going to be a long and gradual process. Have patience with, and respect for, yourself.

This summarizes and highlights what I have found to be an effective means of fostering improvement in speaking behavior, and maximizing the possibility of attaining a workable solution to your problem. Good Luck!

Chapter **8**

overcoming fear and tension in stuttering

James L. Aten

Most people talk without much difficulty most of the time. It's true that people hesitate and stumble over words at times, especially when under stress or fatigue, but they show little concern over such mistakes. What, then, makes your speech different and what can you do to help yourself? Invariably, the person who stutters overreacts to his mistakes. He fears they will occur, becomes tense and feels helpless. During the time that tension is so high, the flow of speech stops or will not start. As you continue to have these tense moments that become different from what normal speakers experience, fear increases to higher and higher levels. You come to dread and perhaps avoid speaking. Many stutterers learn that their greatest enemies are *fear* and *tension*. If the battle with stuttering is to be won, fear and tension must be gradually eliminated. Let's look at

> Fear and tension must be gradually eliminated.

some battle plans that have helped quite a few stutterers conquer the majority of their fears, eliminate excessive tensions, and find that speech in most situations can once again come easily.

Conquering Fear. We have all probably heard that the way to eliminate fear is to "just face up to it." We have learned all too slowly that for some stutterers, fear may actually increase rather than decrease if they continue to face fear situations and fail.

They may experience the same old tension, and fail to get the word out, while attempting to "just go ahead and face their fears." For most of you, fear grew because of repeated failure and the resulting embarrassment over that failure. Your *hope* is that fear can be unlearned by handling hard words and situations better. Performance builds *realistic confidence* that can become a substitute for fear. Here's one way: *Substitute Positive Planning for Fear and Anticipated Failure.*

Stuttering (the fear and tension build-up part) usually begins much earlier in time than you normally think. When the phone rings, you may get into a tense and helpless state while going to answer it. The trouble doesn't suddenly begin as you start to say "Hello." You have learned that tricks such as delaying or rushing often let you down, and so your fear spirals upward. When told that you have a job interview in two days, you often begin worrying about how you'll do and expect failure. Having failed last time, you probably will again unless you plan a new approach to the task:

1. Picture yourself approaching the person who will be interviewing you. Take a breath, then *let* it all go. This feels good and for the first time you experience the condition your speech musculature should be in if words are to come out without tension.

2. Imagine extending your hand slowly to shake hands. Your body movements are slow and confident ones. This reduces the tendency to rush or force speech. Mentally you are calmer. The employer says, "Hello, I'm John Wood. You must be...." Just thinking about answering this with your first and last name fills you with fear and you feel your breath tighten.

3. *LET GO* of that tight breath. Think about the easy movements you could make in answering "Hi, I'm Ed Jones." At first just picture the movements, then after that initial surge of fear subsides, try answering with a kind of easy, half-sigh-like *"Hi"*—Pause—easy again—"I'm *Ed*"—Pause again—let tension go—easy onset—"Jones."

As you rehearse this, several things begin to happen. First, you begin to see that there is less to fear if you don't jump and answer with your first name, which is usually very hard for you.

Second, as one stutterer in our field has said, "Time must become your Friend." You will learn that "haste makes waste," even though a few times in the past it has worked.

Fear won't go away by just waiting or going slower; you have to do some positive planning and desensitizing yourself to the employer's presence and request. You must practice the introduction many times and not just alone but with someone. After you have experienced success alone, ask your wife or friend to be the employer and rehearse. First answer silently, then softly, then in a normal voice. Whether you stutter during the interview or not is of lesser importance. The chances are you will approach the situation easier than you have in a long time and that your actual stuttering will be less severe. New approaches to handling the feared situation bring gradual improvement by reducing fear. This comes through hard work, not magic, pills, tricks, or waiting until you "feel better." The same type of practice and rehearsal can be used in preparing to say "Hello" on the telephone. In fact, you may find the phone less fear-inducing and want to try it first, or, perhaps just greeting someone casually. As one stutterer said, "I try not to go out and put myself into a very difficult situation at first, where I know I'm going to fail." He had learned to approach some situations, though obviously not all of them, by thinking about responding the new easier, relaxed way, and with practice found that he had lost much of his fear. Less fear means less tension in speech.

Conquering Tension. You must learn to substitute easy, slower, more relaxed movements for rushed, tight, forced movements. Typical tension sites are your chest and breath, your throat and vocal cords, jaw, lips and tongue. The practice suggested here can make for

> Substitute easy, slower, more relaxed movements for rushed, tight, forced movements.

success in reducing the fear that follows from blocked movements, so think of these as stages of therapy that you can "put together" for greater effect.

Choose some words that begin with sounds that you think of as being hard—those on which you often stutter. Speech normally begins with a relaxed, unconscious flow of breath.

Practice sighing and letting voice come easily. You don't make voice, it just happens if you will *let* it. The same is true of sounds you make with tongue and lips. Feel yourself gently close the lips for the "P" or move the tongue to form such sounds as "T" and "K," then go ahead and say the rest of the word. Notice how little effort speaking takes. Fear has resulted in too much forcing to get words out. You must learn what 'not forcing' is, and practice until easy movements become habitual. First, practice at a very soft, almost silent level, then gradually at a normal voice level. Practice the movement gently to make the difficult word begin easier, then work on other words that begin with that same movement. Assuming that you engage faithfully in daily practice, try a different sound each week. Fear of words lessens as you repeatedly prove to yourself you have a new, easy way of producing them that is becoming automatic. As you practice, be sure not to let the tongue, lips, vocal cords, or breath become tight or touch too hard. No word or speech movement requires conscious effort. Feel the relaxed easy movements into and out of words. *Stop* and begin the easy movements again for the next word series. Now, you are talking in phrases that are short and that you have confidence you can initiate, if you remember to use the easy beginning you have practiced. Remember, speech sounds better in short phrases with frequent pauses.

By conquering fear-arousal through learning to plan your approach, and then using the easy movements which keep tension from making you feel helpless, you are beginning to control stuttering rather than letting it rule you. Certain speaking situations become easier. At this point you must begin to integrate your success. That is, you are not just *having* good and bad days, you are creating some successes out of potential failure. That's what building confidence is all about—and stutterers say time after time, "I talk better when I'm more confident." When you have created a better performance, you can realistically feel more confidence. The model is then begun for turning 'bad cycles' into good ones. You are then able to turn your attention to fluency rather than frequent expectation of stuttering. One of our adult stutterers who successfully went through the above said, "Now I think more about my fluent successes, and does that ever help!"

You appreciate most in life those things you do for yourself. Getting over stuttering takes tremendous self-discipline and desire. We have found that just practicing easy movements without trying to reduce fear is not too successful, since high fear keeps you from remembering the new easier speech movements at the time when you most need to use them. Also, just trying to reduce fear without giving you something to do that is new—*and that works*—may simply allow fear to creep back into the situation very quickly. We have seen that the majority of the stutterers we work with, using the above procedures, achieve a significant degree of fluency in most situations.

Chapter **9**

don't ever give up!

Peter R. Ramig

Many speech-language pathologists including myself believe that stuttering results from an inherited predisposition or susceptibility to stutter. But I also believe, as do the majority of my colleagues, that the most disabling aspect of stuttering results from our attempts not to stutter.

When we forcibly try to move off and away from the stuttering block, we make it worse. These often futile attempts not to stutter become automatic learned patterns that become strongly conditioned over time. They create stumbling blocks along the road to recovery for many people who stutter.

It is what we do in our attempts not to stutter (i.e., to avoid, conceal, and/or release ourselves from stuttering) that often results in an increase in severity and feelings of helplessness.

Why do so many people who stutter attempt to remediate stuttering using such destructive self-reinforcing strategies? For most of us, feeling different from others is uncomfortable.

> Feeling different from others is uncomfortable.

We react to the perplexed looks, reactions, and the imagined or real scorn of others with feelings of frustration, embarrassment, and shame.

46

A natural physical response to such emotional discomfort is muscular tension, which is a correlate of stress that often makes stuttering worse. When we feel stuck and at the same time embarrassed, we often react with increased muscular effort in our desire to escape the moment of stuttering and move on. It is these reactions, that we learn over time, that create more struggle and tension which often results in more stuttering.

These are the behaviors we can learn to change if we are willing to identify what they are, how we use them in our attempts to escape or avoid stuttering, and how they interfere with the talking process. These are the behaviors I want to encourage you to change. In doing so, you will become more fluent because you will have learned to confront your stuttering without as much fear and trepidation, and thus with less of the confounding muscular effort that often fuels your blocks.

The lesson here is this: The less we try to hide and conceal our stuttering, the more we can learn to stutter with less effort. When this happens, we can become much more in control of our stuttering. In turn we can become more fluent.

The Process of Self-Initiated Recovery

A first step is facing the realization that our stuttering is unlikely to magically disappear on its own. We must come to grips with the fact it will take some perseverance and determination to change the way we have stuttered over the years. Although this may sound difficult or impossible at first, constructively working at changing stuttering often demands less effort and frustration than continuing to fear it. We expend enormous energy in attempts to hide it, and/or push and force through it. And this increases the feelings of helplessness in the wake of its presence. Because I am convinced that stuttering can be changed with determination and self-initiated effort, I want to briefly outline some additional factors we can use in our efforts to weaken and even completely undermine stuttering.

Producing speech is a highly complex process.

Understand the Physical Speaking Process

Producing speech is a highly complex process. However, paying attention to how we physically use our tongue, lips, and voice box as we produce sounds can help us understand how we often create more stuttering. We do this by tensing and forcing these structures as we attempt to deal with the unpleasant moments of stuttering. Of course these speech structures consist of muscles that need to be tensed to a normal degree in order to produce fluent speech.

In contrast, however, people who stutter often tense these muscles excessively, block, and then push forcibly to "break" through the block in their urgency to release themselves from the feeling of being stuck. This pattern develops over time as a reaction to the little understood core cause(s) of stuttering, or what some of us refer to as the "stuttering trigger." In essence, the stuttering trigger is the present cause of stuttering. It may be associated with the inherited predisposition to be dysfluent that is found in the small percentage of the population who stutter. But that doesn't mean it can't be dealt with.

Once we begin to pay attention to our speech structures, we can better understand how we interfere with their normal functioning during stuttering. We can then feel how pushing our lips together using excessive tension creates and/or makes stuttering worse by closing off the air and voicing necessary for speech production. We can then begin to work at producing sounds with less pushing and forcing as we move our lips, tongue, and voice box. This increases our chances of stuttering with less effort and severity. As we further develop and refine these monitoring skills, we will not only produce easier forms of stuttering, but we will become more fluent as we are less likely to "pull the stuttering trigger."

Try Not to Recoil From Stuttering — Instead, Move Forward

Once we understand the importance of eliminating much of the pushing and forcing in our tongue, lips, and voice box, we can begin to stutter more audibly and effortlessly by holding on to the stuttering moment while moving forward to the next sound.

When we work at stuttering audibly, we are better able to turn on and continue our air and voicing: two of the primary ingredients necessary for the production of normal speech. In contrast, due to the embarrassment and frustration often associated with stuttering, many people who stutter have learned to block silently at the tongue, lips, or vocal cords and/or recoil repetitively from their blocks and other dysfluent moments.

Attempting to speak in this manner interrupts both the flow of air and the necessary voicing created by vibrating vocal cords. This common process of trying to conceal and minimize the audible stuttering actually complicates speaking and over time, often increases the visibility and severity of stuttering.

Keeping the air and voicing turned on when we stutter takes time and practice at first because we are forcing ourselves to confront something that feels and sounds unpleasant and abnormal. Yet it is a necessary step in the process of learning to stutter in a forward fashion. It will also help you in changing harder stuttering to easier and less frequent stuttering.

Pay Attention to Feeling How and Where Your Lips, Tongue, and Voice Box Make Specific Sounds

Once we have learned how the physical speaking mechanism functions, and we have worked on lessening our recoil behaviors, we can then begin to concentrate on how it feels to make the sounds and words as we speak. The vast majority of people cue into the sound of their speech as they talk. There is scientific evidence that auditory "cues" can be a present cause of stuttering. In contrast, many of us encourage people who stutter to focus on the "feel" of speaking and less to listening to their speech.

A way to begin to learn this process is to close your eyes as you say words and short phrases over and over again, concentrating on visualizing and feeling the movement and touch of your lips, tongue, and vocal cords. Next, practice cuing into the feel of these structures as you purposely push hard during speaking. Then, contrast your hard talking with how it feels to touch lightly with the lips, tongue, and vocal cords.

These "compare-contrast exercises" facilitate learning to monitor your speech by feel. Then, after you begin to realize you are able to "feel" your production of sounds and phrases, you are encouraged to practice feeling your speech more generally as you practice speaking using longer connected sentences. This task may seem very foreign at first, but with practice and time, it becomes easier and can be accomplished with less effort.

Open Your Mouth When You Talk

In order to counteract the tendency to stifle mouth opening as you talk, practice deliberate mouth opening as you repeat the

Figure 1. Self Initiated Steps in the Process of
Recovery From Stuttering

sequence outlined above. The tendency for persons who stutter
to "clench" or reduce mouth opening is a problem I find
necessary to address when working with many adolescents and
adults. This "clenching tendency" is actually reduced mouth
opening that we learn over time as a result of our anticipating
difficult sounds or words. This physical change in mouth
opening (clenching) seems to result from the process of "holding
back" the stuttering.

In a Matter of Fact Manner
Acknowledge That You Stutter

We know that people who stutter often view their stuttering
as embarrassing and shameful. As a result of such perceptions,
we may shroud our stuttering in a "conspiracy of silence."
Unsurprisingly, family, friends, and co-workers know we stutter,
and are usually unsure of whether or not to maintain eye contact,
look away, or fill in the words, etc. Such uncertainty may create
uneasiness and discomfort in our listeners as well as ourselves.

However, much of the uneasiness and uncertainty
experienced by both of us can be significantly reduced by
acknowledging in an open and matter of fact manner that we
stutter. For example, say something as simple as, "By the way,
I'm going to use this opportunity to practice some speech
techniques I've been working on lately. This is not an easy chore,
but I know you understand why it is important for me to take
this opportunity to practice as we speak."

This sample remark gives our listeners an opportunity to ask questions about stuttering, a communication problem that many people find intriguing. If we choose, it also gives us an opportunity to talk about it and "gives us permission" to openly practice some of the steps outlined in this chapter and throughout this book. Disclosure is a proactive strategy that affords us the opportunity to address our stuttering in a matter of fact and nonchalant manner. Doing so increases our comfort level because we begin to view our problem in a more positive light. This new perception eventually facilitates changing our view of stuttering as the "shameful unmentionable."

Confront Stuttering By Occasionally Inserting Pseudostuttering in Your Fluent Speech

Many people who stutter cringe at the first suggestion that they should occasionally purposely insert a prolonged or repeated sound as they speak. Paradoxically, the voluntary insertion of mild, easy "stuttering" can be helpful in your quest to lessen your fear and apprehension of stuttering. Although you will hear yourself do this, listeners are usually much less aware of what you are doing because your voluntary dysfluencies are short and produced without excessive tension. Those who are recovering from stuttering often cite this task as one that helped them maintain their improvement during their recovery process.

Never give up!

As stated earlier, changing stuttering requires persistence and determination. However, our recovery process actually demands less effort, struggle, and embarrassment than the negative emotionality experienced when we live a life focused on hiding, concealing, and fighting stuttering. Hiding or fighting requires a huge amount of vigilance and surveillance, and this only tends to feed the destructive stuttering cycle. I have known many people who stutter, clients I have personally worked with and colleagues and professionals I have learned from, who have made substantial gains in releasing themselves from the handicapping grip of stuttering. Many have become so fluent that most people are unaware they sometimes still stutter.

This was my dream. This was their dream. This can realistically be your dream.

basic goals for a person who stutters

J. David Williams

I can't tell you how to stop stuttering, which is what you would like. But there are ways that you can stutter more easily, which sound better and make you more comfortable with your speech, and make a better impression on your listener. Listeners react to the way you appear to be reacting to yourself. If you seem to be tense, panicky, and out of control, they will also feel tense, to which you react by becoming more tense and hurried yourself. It's a circular process that you can learn to control.

The basic idea is to do all of your stuttering with less struggle, tension, and panic. This doesn't mean to talk more slowly in an effort to avoid all stuttering. Go ahead and speak at your normal rate, but when you feel that you are about to block on a word, slow down at that point and take your time saying the feared

> Resist any feeling of hurry or pressure.

word. Don't give up your effort to say the word, but try to stutter easily and slowly. Relax and let go: keep your lips, tongue and jaw moving gently without jamming. Don't panic. Take all the time you need. Concentrate on confidence and sense of control.

Keep moving forward but move slowly and positively. Resist any feeling of hurry or pressure. At some instant you will know that you are over the hump. Simply finish that word and keep talking along at your usual rate until you start to tense up again for another feared word. Then instantly shift into slow motion again. Many stutterers who originally had very tense, complex patterns of stuttering have worked themselves down to this easy, simple, slow stuttering with little tension or interruption in their speech.

Another technique that I have always found helpful, and used to practice a great deal, is to deliberately repeat the initial sound or syllable of a word on which I felt I might stutter. I made one or several deliberate repetitions before I even tried to utter the word as a whole. The effect was to give me a feeling of control. The listener might think I was really stuttering, but I was not. I was being deliberately disfluent to eliminate any fear of stuttering at that instant. Rather than giving way to panic, tension and struggle, I was doing on purpose something that I usually tried desperately to avoid doing. And it really worked. This technique weakened my fear of stuttering and I felt a delicious freedom and control. It's an old, old idea: if you are terrified of doing a particular thing, your fear will decrease in proportion to your ability to do at least part of the feared behavior deliberately. And whatever else stuttering is, it is behavior that is increased by your fearful, struggling efforts to avoid doing it. The more I sidestepped uncontrolled tension by throwing in occasional deliberate disfluencies (repetitions or prolongations of sounds) the less I really stuttered.

Deliberate disfluency is a simple thing to do, but you may recoil in horror at the very idea. You may say, "People will think I'm stuttering if I do that!" It's amazing how we who stutter can hold on to our illusions. We hate and fear stuttering, and try desperately not to stutter. We develop a repertoire of complex denial and avoidance attitudes and behaviors. So the idea of being deliberately disfluent, or publicly displaying what we have spent so much time and energy trying to hide, seems to make no sense. In reality it makes a great deal of sense, but you have to begin to convince yourself of that. People may think you are stuttering when you are being deliberately disfluent, but what do they think when they see and hear you doing your real stuttering? Think about this a bit, and perhaps ask a friend or two their opinion.

As you well know, when you stutter you feel out of control. You are struggling to regain control. The operative word is "struggling." The more you feel you have to struggle to say a word, the more you are out of control. So anything you do deliberately to reduce tension when expecting to stutter or actually stuttering increases your control. You cannot stutter deliberately; you can only pretend to stutter. So the more you are deliberately disfluent, the less you will actually stutter.

It takes practice to start accepting this idea. Try it first when you are alone. Then try it in easy, non-threatening situations, and analyze your feelings. As you begin to feel more comfortable with your deliberate disfluency try doing it more and more, and in gradually tougher speaking situations. It is very likely to decrease your fear and increase your natural, inherent fluency.

There is no one way to speak, or to handle your stuttering, that is going to guarantee fluency within any specified length of time. The primary goal is to have a feeling that you are actively doing things that decrease your fear of stuttering and give you a sense of control. It's great to realize that whenever you stutter, there is something you can do about it — relax and delay your stuttering behaviors, introduce some deliberate disfluency to counteract your tendency to panic, or change your pattern of stuttering in any manner that allows you to communicate more comfortably without trying to be perfectly fluent. If you are like most people who stutter, you are much more intolerant of your own "speech failures" than are your listeners. It took me a long time to learn that other people really didn't care whether I stuttered or not. They liked me or they didn't, but my stuttering had very little to do with it.

There is still much speculation about the basic cause and nature of stuttering, but one thing is clear: your fear of it is the most disruptive and toughest aspect to deal with. If you weren't afraid of stuttering, you would not have tried so hard and so ineffectively

> Your fear is the most disruptive and toughest aspect to deal with.

to deny, conceal, and avoid its occurrence. Fear disrupts rational thinking and voluntary motor behavior, including speech. If your fear of stuttering reaches a critical level at any given moment, it becomes literally impossible for you to carry out any voluntary speech modification techniques you have learned, and you'll probably stutter as badly as ever.

So an important goal is to learn to keep your fear of stuttering within manageable limits. Try not to give way to blind panic at the approach of a feared speaking situation. You cannot just wish away your old, well-conditioned fear responses, but you can practice overriding the fear. It is always better to go ahead and talk even if you stutter, rather than to remain silent for fear of stuttering. This gives you just a bit more courage the next time!

In practicing changes in your way of stuttering and in reducing your fear of stuttering, you must be "actively patient." Stuttering did not develop overnight, and you're not going to make permanent changes overnight. Keep in mind that you don't **cure** behavior, you **change** it. There is no known universally effective medicine for the cure of stuttering. There is only a learning process: learning how to change your speech behavior in desirable ways, and how to develop the right attitudes toward that behavior. Real and permanent change in feelings and behaviors does not happen easily, quickly, or automatically. You have to be active and repeatedly do things that bring about the results you want. You have to be patient. Improvement will come in direct proportion to the amount of active, sustained, daily effort you expend. Many small successes cumulate to produce a more permanent change than does one spectacular event.

Apart from the specific things you can do about your stuttering problem, such as modifying your speaking pattern and reducing your fear and avoidance, there is a more general and more basic goal. You need to increase your self-esteem and to enjoy life to the fullest. Stuttering is never fun, but it is only a part of your life, one of many parts. Keep it in perspective. Have a real-

Capitalize on all your personal assets, your skills and talents.

istic view of the ways in which it may be a handicap and the more numerous ways in which it is not. Develop and capitalize on all your personal assets, your skills and talents. The happier you are in general, the more self-fulfilled you'll feel, and the less important your stuttering will become.

Identify with people, and accept the fact that you are a qualified member of the human race. Have an "approach" rather than an "avoidance" attitude toward others. Remember that everyone has feelings of inadequacy and insecurity for one reason or another, no matter how they appear in public. An emotional common denominator among all people is much more likely to be anxiety and a sense of inadequacy rather than supreme self-confidence and superiority. Anxiety and feelings of worthlessness keep you from enjoying life. They diminish positive, outward-looking attitudes, and practically wipe out any healthy sense of humor.

Way back, I did a good deal of self-modification of my stuttering, and I gradually overcame much of my fear, shame and avoidance. Slowly, with many ups and downs, I became more fluent and I enjoyed life more and more. I became aware that I was making phone calls without thinking twice about them, and speaking easily in many other situations that used to make me break out in a cold sweat. It felt wonderful, and still does when I stop to think about it. Mostly I just communicate with people without fear or struggle. I still stutter slightly, but it has long ceased to be a real problem. Occasionally, after one speaking situation or another, I'll think, "Gee, that used to scare the hell out of me." Then I go back to confronting other and more immediate problems that are the inevitable concomitants of age. Stuttering fades to insignificance.

I have no regrets other than the time and energy I wasted feeling sorry for myself because I stuttered. I think I would have progressed faster in coping with my stuttering problem if I had available the kind of valid, useful literature now produced by the Stuttering Foundation. I encourage all people who stutter to read everything they can about stuttering. In this way they will gradually increase their ability to distinguish between facile promises of unattainable "miracle cures" and solid, time-tested ideas and methods of self-improvement.

As a final suggestion, join or form a mutual-support, self-help group for people who stutter. There are several such groups in America, Europe and elsewhere. They increase motivation for self-therapy, provide social reinforcement and an opportunity for members to learn from one another. I have enjoyed and benefited from such activities for many years.

Chapter 11

some suggestions for those who want to talk easily

Dean E. Williams

For purposes of this paper, I want you to assume that I am meeting with a group of people who stutter for the first time and that you are a member of that group. My purpose will be to suggest what I think you can do to improve the ways you talk. The major points presented in this paper are those that would be discussed and elaborated and experienced during the subsequent weeks of therapy. It is important to point out that I am talking to you as a *group*; for any one person in the group, I would direct my attention toward his own special feelings, viewpoints and needs. Because this discussion is directed toward a group, it will be necessary for each of you to think through the comments made and to apply them to your own individual problem.

In working to solve a problem such as stuttering, you must first ponder the various ways that you think about the problem for they affect, in good part, what you do as you talk. They affect the observations you make, the ways you react inside, and the ways you interpret the success or failure of what you have done. Furthermore, they determine, in the main, what you will do the next time you talk.

Think about your stuttering problem. *How* do you view it? *What* do you do that you call your stuttering? *Why* do you think you do it? *What* are the most helpful things you can do when you stutter? *How* do they relate to what you believe is wrong? *What* does not help? Why? When one begins to ask questions about what he is doing, it can stimulate him to make observations about his behavior. This, in turn, encourages him to become *involved* with the ways he feels, with the ways he thinks, and with what he is doing as he talks. This is necessary! You cannot solve a problem by acting like an innocent bystander waiting for someone else to answer questions that you never thought to ask. It is *your* problem and you must face it. Perhaps I can help stimulate you to consider your own beliefs by relating examples of how a few other stutterers of different ages have viewed their stuttering. In my opinion, the ways they talk about the problem change in relation to the number of years they have attempted to cope with it.

The seven-to-nine-year-old stutterer is apt to be confused and bewildered by the ways he talks and by people's reactions to it. One second grade boy reported that when he was in kindergarten and first grade he had repeated sounds a great deal. People called it "stuttering." Now, he tensed and "pushed" to get the words out so he wouldn't "repeat," or "stutter," as he understood the meaning of the word. Now, people were calling the tensing and pushing "stuttering." He was confused!

A 9-year-old typically held his breath, blinked his eyes and tensed his jaw. This, to him, was his stuttering. One day he began taking quick breaths and then blurting the word out quickly. He reported that he was doing this so he wouldn't do the holding of breath and other behavior mentioned above. People were still reacting to that as "stuttering." He was bewildered. The children were doing certain behaviors in order to "help them get the words out," and those behaviors were called stuttering. When they did something else in order to not do those behaviors, people also were calling that stuttering too. Their only recourse, then, was to do something else so they wouldn't do what they just did. Does this sound confusing? It was confusing to the children too! Yet, one can observe the same behavior in adults. When was the last time that you did something similar, for example jerking your head backwards, so you would not tense your jaw and prolong a sound?

Children in their early teens often report more magical beliefs about stuttering than do the younger children. When some 12 or 13-year-olds were asked to discuss the question "What is stuttering like?" one 13-year-old boy reported that it is like trying to ride an untamed horse. He worried about when it (the "stuttering horse") would shy away from a word, would balk at the sight of a word or would begin to "buck" on a word. He felt that the only thing he could do was hang on as hard as he could, keep a tight rein on the horse and just "hope" that the horse wouldn't be too violent. Another 13-year-old reported that talking was like Indian wrestling. He constantly had to strain and to struggle so that his opponent (his stuttering) didn't get the best of him. As he talked, he tried to overpower it. The children talked as if they had to fight against their "stutter." Their "stuttering" was an adversary with a mind of its own, and in most instances, they were afraid that it was stronger than they were. With this viewpoint, then, it is quite natural for the child to feel that he has to tense, to struggle, and to use his muscles to fight the "stutter." It has been my observation that adults who stutter generally do the same thing, although they may not explain so vividly the reasons for doing it.

As adults, you probably have stuttered for many more years than the children just discussed. Whereas they still are actively trying to "explain" to themselves the reasons why they tense and struggle, you may have forgotten to ask "Why?" anymore. You no longer question the necessity or helpfulness of doing the tensing or head jerking or eye blinking that you do. You just accept it as part of what you, as a stutterer, *have to do* to talk. This is unfortunate because then you do not direct your attention toward observing, studying, and experimenting with what you can do in order to talk without the tensing and struggling. Yet, you can learn to talk easily and effortlessly.

There is nothing inside your body that will stop you from talking. You have the same speaking equipment as anyone else.

You are doing things to interfere with talking because you think they help.

You have the ability to talk normally. You are doing things to interfere with talking because you think they help. You tense the muscles of your chest, throat, mouth, etc., in an effort to try and fight the "stutter." Yet these are the same muscles that you need to use in order to talk. You can't do both at the same time because you only have one set of muscles. Therefore, it is extremely helpful to begin studying what normal speakers do as they talk. This is what you want to learn to do. Observe carefully the way they move their mouth, lips and jaws as they are talking. Then, sit and talk in a room by yourself, or read in unison with someone else and study the feeling of movement as you talk. There is a certain "just right tensing" that you do as you move your jaw and tongue and lips. Study it! This is what you want to do when you talk. Now begin to look at what you do to interfere with talking when you do what you refer to as your "stuttering." If you begin to hold your breath or tense your jaw, for example, you cannot move as easily as you must do to talk the way normal speakers do. In short, you need to develop a sharp sense of contrast between what you are doing that you call "stuttering" and what you do as you just talk easily. Use a mirror or a tape recorder to help you observe what you are doing. Above all, get a feeling deep in your muscles of the movements involved in easy talking. Then you can become much more alert to what you are *doing* (not what's "happening" to you) as you tense and interfere with talking.

After careful observation and practice of what you do as you talk easily and on-goingly, as opposed to interfering with talking by tensing, stopping, or speeding, etc., enter a few speaking situations that are not so threatening that you cannot observe your behavior. It has been my experience that ordinarily the person observes that he gets scared, or he gets a "feeling" that he was going to stutter, and he tenses. What is this feeling? Work to be able to tolerate it so you can observe it carefully. Enter more speaking situations. Answer some questions. To what is the feeling similar? Does the feeling *alone* make you unable to talk? Or, do you tense when you begin to experience the feeling? When you start to talk do you pay attention to what you want to do (the movement you want to make) or are you attending to the "feeling" waiting for it to tell you whether you will be able to talk or note? Study the feeling. If you study it in various situations as you are talking you will become aware that it is a feeling that is in no way special from any other feeling of fear or embarrassment, etc. It is very normal. However, it is a feeling to which you have learned to react by tensing, or by speeding or slowing your rate. Essentially, you react to it by *doing* extra muscular activity than is necessary to do in order to talk. When you become aware that the struggling behavior you call stuttering is something that you are *doing* as you talk, and not something that magically "happens to you," you are in a very good position to begin to change what you are doing as you talk so that you can talk easier. Then, you can begin to talk by starting to move easily, being willing to experience the feelings that you may feel, but to continue moving easily. You can tolerate a few bobbles as you do this. Then, you can begin to see that there is a way out of this jungle. There is a reason to become optimistic because it is within your ability to do it. It's essentially a problem of learning to just "let yourself talk." You have learned to do too much. You do things to interfere. Learn by observing and experimenting that these things do not help. Talking is essentially easy ongoing movement of the jaw, tongue and lips, etc. Tensing unnecessarily only gets in your way. Your success in countering the excessive tensing as you talk will depend upon two factors. The first involves the thoroughness with which you come to understand that there is

> Talking is essentially easy ongoing movement of the jaw, tongue and lips, etc.

no "stuttering" to be *fought, avoided or controlled*, other than the tensing you, yourself, perform. Once you understand this as you talk, your own tensing becomes a signal for you to begin reacting constructively by immediately easing off on the tensing and attending to the easy on-goingness of talking.

The second involves practice. You must practice talking easily as you would practice typing or playing the piano easily and on-goingly even though you had a feeling in your stomach or chest that you might "goof" it at some point. Then, expand your speaking situations—and practice—until you can talk comfortably at any time you choose to speak.

This is the beginning of therapy for you. From now on, it is up to you!

Chapter 12

suggestions for self-therapy for stutterers

Margaret M. Neely

Dear Fellow-Stutterer: If you are an adult who has stuttered most of your life, you have probably tried many ways to cope with the problem. So have I. As a stutterer and a therapist, my observation is that each person finds his own way. There are a multitude of approaches to the correction of stuttering. The procedure I suggest is not necessarily the "best" approach; it is simply an approach that has been effective for me and for most of the individuals with whom I have worked. It is a direct attack on the speech and it involves effort. Many people resist the work aspect and want easier ways to overcome the problem. The feelings of anxiety that accompany stuttering have become so overwhelming that the stutterer reacts by wanting a simple way with immediate results. Drug therapy to relieve anxiety and mechanical devices to block your own hearing or to supply you with rhythmic patterns are easy methods which seem immediately beneficial. I believe that nothing succeeds on a long term basis like hard work on the speech itself, an idea that may be due to the very personal viewpoint of anyone who is both a therapist and a stutterer. My own experience has been that nothing "cures" an adult stutterer, but one can effectively manage stuttering so that it ceases to be a significant problem throughout one's life.

Why does this approach require work? Because speech, like walking and other body functions, is acquired early in life and becomes habitual long before school age. Those of us who stutter have learned both fluent and stuttered forms of speech which have become automatic. You, as a stutterer, must study your speech patterns in order to become aware of the differences between stuttered and fluent speech. Stuttered forms of speech can be changed in various ways, just as handwriting can be modified.

Stuttered forms of speech can be changed.

It is this changing of an established habit that requires work.

Several psychological problems confront the stutterer as he tries to alter his speech. These problems include a lack of confidence in his ability to do anything with his stuttered speech because of previous failures, an inability to cope with feelings of resentment and loneliness about having this problem (why me?), and worry and concern about the effect of his stuttering on other people and their possible resulting opinions of him. In addition, the stutterer struggles with the idea that because he can say his words fluently some of the time, he should be able to say them fluently all of the time. He may believe some psychological problem needs to be removed, and this belief results either in periodic over-worry about his speech or complete disregard for it. These feelings which have become automatic, as has the stuttering, usually are the painful part of stuttering. This is why you may feel the need to first work on eliminating the feelings you experience when you stutter. However, it is easier to work on the speech first, and the feeling next, because much of the accompanying emotion disappears when you have gained control of your speech.

How do you start?

Your goal should be to find a way of speaking that is comfortable for you. You will need to eliminate the abnormality of your stuttering and try to find an easier way to talk which is under your control.

Study your speech. Learn to change the habitual form of stuttering to a more controlled pronunciation of the word. Change your speech to include fluent speech, pauses and the controlled saying of words, as well as occasional stuttering.

To study your speech, analyze how you say words both fluently and in a stuttered form. You may think of a word as being a unit or "lump" of sound; actually a word is composed of separate sounds, much as a written word consists of separate letters. To say a word you must move from sound position to sound position with your speech articulators shaping the air that carries the voice. Learn to be aware of the feeling of muscle action as you move through a word. When a word is said fluently these muscular movements are coordinated, loose and easy.

> Analyze how you say words both fluently and in a stuttered form.

When you stutter, you will notice that there is a great deal of tension in the speech muscles used to say the beginning sound. Much of the abnormality of stuttering is your automatic reaction to the feeling of the sudden muscle tension that you experience as a "blocked" feeling. You try to fight the blocking by pushing harder, rather than by releasing the tension and moving to the rest of the word. As you say an isolated word beginning with a B or P, for example, concentrate on the feeling of movement as you bring your lips together and as they move to the next sounds. In the habitual stuttering pattern the muscles will either tighten and then release to bounce back to the same position, or will jerk forward to the rest of the word. This is in contrast to a fluent saying of the first sound which will have loose contact of the lips and a smooth shift to the next sound position.

Study your conversational speech. You may stutter more in connected speech than when you say single words. Such factors as the speed of speaking and word position in a sentence can influence how a word is said, and can precipitate stuttering. Stutterers have a good deal of fluent speech as well as stuttered speech. Learn to be aware of the feeling of fluency and the sensation of fast, easy movement of the muscles involved in speech. These movements are interrupted only to take a breath, or to pause for meaning. When a pause for stuttering occurs, you may notice that the rate of speech increases after the block as if to "make up" for lost time. Sometimes this increased speed produces a rapid, jerky speech pattern that is difficult to understand. Stutterers usually hurry in their speech more than normal speakers do. You may want to consider changing the rate of both your fluent and your stuttered speech.

How do you practice changing the habitual form of stuttering to a controlled pronunciation of words?

Begin with single words. Watch in a mirror as you place your mouth in position to say the first sound of the word. Move slowly and gently from sound to sound through the word. Practice this silently, whispering, and then aloud as you learn to feel the sensation of relaxed movements of the lips, tongue, and throat. Through awareness of muscle movement you can control your speech production even when talking to other people and are unable to use a mirror.

Read aloud to yourself. Say each word in the sentence as if it were an isolated word. Be highly conscious of the feeling of movement through the word.

Practice saying words directly using a talking-and-writing technique. Write the first letter of the word as you begin to say the word and prolong the first sound until you have completed the written letter. This slow first movement of the word will train you to combat the excessive muscle tension which automatically occurs at the beginning of stuttered words.

Try to learn a new speech pattern which can be used in every day speaking. You may have noticed that one of the important factors which influences the amount of stuttering in your everyday speech is your feeling of inner stability. This feeling is what you experience as self-confidence, calmness and self-control. Many influences from the environment, or from your physical state, can affect your equilibrium. Most of these environmental influences are beyond your control. However, you can change to a speech pattern that is under your voluntary control, rather than responding to the pressures with habitual tense and stuttered speech. This pattern should consist of your fluent speech, which you refuse to hurry, and your careful, relaxed, controlled speech. By using your awareness of muscle movement to guide your lips, tongue, and throat from sound to sound throughout the word, much as in writing, you can reduce much of the abnormality and tension that occurs in a stuttered word. Use of this controlled pronunciation on some of the fluent words as well as the stuttered words can keep a smooth speech pattern. This takes work, but can become habitual in many situations. Your over-all goal is to find a way of speaking that is comfortable for you. This should include the following ideas:

1. Acceptance of the idea that you are a "controlled" stutterer rather than a fluent speaker.

2. Awareness of the "feel" of shaping words fluently.

3. Mastery of the panic of stuttering will occur when you accept, as normal for you, the pauses and moments of tension that occur in your speech. By reducing the struggle of stuttering you relieve yourself of embarrassment, but you cannot hurry when stuttering.

4. Self-discipline in daily practice.

5. Humor as you look at your mistakes in speaking. Many things about stuttering can be funny.

Stuttering is a life-long problem which improves with age. As a stutterer you can gain great satisfaction in watching yourself acquire better and better control of speech as you work on it.

Chapter **13**

self-improvement after unsuccessful treatments

Henry Freund

Like most adult stutterers in this country you have probably been subjected to some form of therapy at one time or another. This therapy was either totally ineffective or resulted in only temporary improvement. Maybe it even resulted in a "cure," only to be followed by a relapse. Such an experience may have provoked in you an attitude of pessimism as far as the possibility of a more effective treatment is concerned. Or, it may have strengthened your desire for the "miracle," the perfect cure which would eradicate every trace of stuttering. Both these attitudes are unjustified.

For those who are pessimistic about the possibility of help, it may be encouraging to learn that some stutterers have been able to help themselves either in spite of, or possibly because of, repeated and unsuccessful treatments. Some of the contributors to this book will give you specific and practical advice about what to do in times of trouble. I want to give you a short description of my own attempts at self-improvement, after many unsuccessful treatments, and the principles on which they were based. This is my own strictly personal way of helping myself and should not be considered as a blueprint to be followed rigidly. Each individual must go his own way.

67

For those who are overly optimistic, a few words of caution are needed. I am intentionally talking only about *improvements* and not about *cures*. I am of the opinion that for the adult stutterer the best we can expect is long-term, even lifelong improvement, which renders him a less unhappy and less socially withdrawn person. This is not a perfect cure. Traces of the disorder usually remain and relapses occur. This applies equally to those who were treated by others and to those who treated themselves.

> I am intentionally talking about *improvements* and not about *cures*.

It seems to me that those "former stutterers" who really don't have any trace of stuttering left did not recover as a result of planning and conscious efforts but actually outgrew their disorder without knowing how and why. Their cure is, as we say, a spontaneous recovery and not the result of therapy.

I was definitely a severe stutterer and was treated unsuccessfully by leading European authorities during my elementary school and high school years, as a student in medical school and even after graduation. Without the knowledge I acquired as a result of all these futile attempts at therapy, however, I probably never would have succeeded in helping myself overcome the worst of my stuttering. As an eight year old child I experienced a short-lived and almost miraculous improvement by using a smooth, melodic manner of speech and prolonged syllables; sentences were uttered as units. It was a manner of speech akin to singing. I noticed that I could apply this method in front of strangers with perfect ease and confidence when accompanied by my therapist. But he accompanied me only rarely, and never made any systematic attempt to enlarge the range of situations I could master. I returned home as "cured," only to relapse quickly. The next two authorities conducted therapy strictly within the walls of their office. The first one, after many tricks and much logical persuasion, finally stumbled upon rhythmic speech; again I felt an almost miraculous ease, but no attempt was made to help me apply this in front of others. The last therapist totally rejected my request to accompany me into real life situations. He wanted me to have the courage to do it alone. My numerous attempts to approach people alone and to conquer my fear of stuttering all

68

ended in failure and my stuttering grew worse. From bitter experience I learned how futile it is to make demands upon the stutterer without giving him a helping hand. What I needed was not an authority but a friend and collaborator genuinely interested in me and ready to help me. I was fortunate to have a brother who could be this friend.

At age 35 I gave up my practice as general practitioner of medicine and moved from Yugoslavia to Berlin for postgraduate training and specialization. My shyness to approach people had reached a point where something had to be done about it, and I was now given an opportunity to make a new start. My chances for a successful attempt at treating myself were favorable. Not only had I accumulated an extensive knowledge on stuttering, but through

> Bridge the gap between theory and practice.

my many unsuccessful treatments in the past I had developed definite ideas of what was necessary to do to bridge the gap between theory and practice. I tried to follow these main principles.

1. I determined to make full use of the opportunity to devote myself completely to the task of self-improvement. The chances of success would be better if I were able to live completely for this one task. I had to make full use of a new environment where nobody knew me as "stutterer" and where nothing reminded me of my past defeats and humiliating experiences.

2. I knew by now that I possessed a normal ability to speak. Speaking is an automatic act and most of the time I did speak normally. I knew that stuttering occurred situationally, that it resulted from fear and the expectation of failure, and that this lead to an inhibition or stoppage of the voice. I talked under the illusion that speech sounds are difficult and that an enormous amount of force was necessary to overcome my self-created obstacles. Talking was a highly emotional experience which gave me a feeling of helplessness, failure and defeat. But I also knew that the method I used as a child which stressed all the positive aspects of speech (the stream of breath and voice, the unity of the sentence as a whole, the singing-like, melodic aspects of speech) was in the past prone to draw my attention away from the dreaded speech sounds, tended to calm and relax me, and rendered my speech more pleasurable. As a first step I would now

start again to use this method with those persons closest to me and regain my old confidence in it. I could use this as a stepping stone to contacts with others.

3. I would discuss with my brother my daily predicaments, fears, doubts, successes, defeats and other personal problems. After establishing a good and trusting relationship I explained my strategy. He should accompany me wherever and whenever I needed his help; he should remain silent when I was sure of myself but should take over when I stumbled; or he could start to talk and then I could gradually take over. In this manner I could slowly expand the variety of people and situations where I could talk methodically, calmly and confidently.

4. After establishing a greater degree of security and confidence I would be able to reduce and finally discard the need for my brother to accompany me. I would be on my own and would expand the range of situations I wanted to master. I would do this gradually and would not ask for too much too soon. In times of trouble, I should not be too proud to discuss my problems with others.

5. Having widened somewhat the range of situations and people that I could handle without fear, I had to secure my newly won abilities by preparing myself for the inevitable reversals. Relapses would be unavoidable and had to be expected, for there would be no foolproof method to eliminate them. In the past relapses were prone to shatter my belief not only in a certain method, but also in ever being able to overcome my stuttering. This would not happen again if I were prepared to meet them in the right spirit. Situations and circumstances would arise when the magical power of any method would be overpowered by old fears and self-doubts, and when some outposts of the liberated area might get again lost. The right spirit to meet relapses and reversals is a philosophy of self-tolerance, of the acceptance of your own weaknesses and limitations, and of a greater objectivity toward self and others. This results in a lessened sensitivity. Here, too, an open discussion with an understanding person sometimes helps to clarify issues which subjectively you are unable to see clearly.

I followed these and other similar guidelines. The breakthrough occurred when, after a period of preparation and accompanied by my brother, I for the first time dared to approach a stranger for the purpose of experimenting on him. In spite of a panic-like fear and desire to run away, I heard myself asking him a question in a surprisingly calm and methodic fashion. This first breakthrough shattered the walls of fear and avoidance. It was a positive emotional experience of strong impact; it created a new confidence and opened up new vistas. The world became a friendlier place to live in and I felt closer to other human beings. Many similar positive experiences followed. My liberated verbal territory became too big to ever again fall prey to the demons of fear and

> This first breakthrough shattered the walls of fear and avoidance.

doubt. For the next six years I spoke practically without conscious fear of stuttering and was able to engage in activities like counseling, lecturing and teaching as head of several speech clinics. These tasks I could not have possibly performed before. Then minor relapses, especially during exceptionally difficult life-situations, started to occur. While traces of the disorder have remained, and while with advancing age I have again become slightly more socially handicapped, the disorder never again assumed the severity it had prior to age 35. But even now, 40 years later, I still not only continue to study myself but also to treat myself. I still work to normalize my relationship to others and on my life-philosophy. For me, this is a lifelong task.

This is my story of self-improvement after unsuccessful treatment. Maybe there are some ideas which will prove helpful to you. I hope so!

Chapter 14

some helpful attitudes underlying success in therapy

Harold L. Luper

It's been more than twenty-five years since I first entered the speech therapy program which proved effective in significantly reducing my speech problem. Much has happened in speech pathology since that time. Although there have been few completely new techniques, the manner of programming these techniques and the manner in which they are applied to persons have continually been improving. Speech pathologists are constantly seeking better ways to help the stutterer, and what's considered best today will probably be replaced in the future with something better. For this reason, I shall not dwell as much on the specific techniques and activities that helped me as upon the general attitudes and principles which seem to underlie successful stuttering therapy.

The Power of Constructive Assertiveness. A few years ago, Norman Vincent Peale popularized a set of attitudes in his book, *The Power of Positive Thinking*. One of the principles that I found of most value in changing my stuttering problem might be called *constructive assertiveness*. Like many of you, one of the most common and most debilitating characteristics of my problem was my habit of avoiding. I continually searched for ways to get around saying words on which I expected to stutter. There was almost no limit to what I would do to avoid situations in which I feared my stuttering would embarrass me. Going to a party would be an extremely tiring event because the entire evening would be spent trying to stay alert for words on which I might stutter and finding ways to avoid saying them.

> There was almost no limit to what I would do to avoid situations.

Fortunately, even before I began active therapy, I found out that avoidance only makes the fear worse. While serving in the army, I had written a speech pathologist asking for help. He informed me he would be glad to see me after I was out of the service and gave me a few suggestions as to what I could do in the meantime. His most important suggestion was to begin to lick the problem of avoidance. He suggested I go ahead and say those words on which I expected to stutter and to go ahead and enter those situations which I normally avoided. I began to try it. It was hard, but soon I found that the temporary discomfort of struggling through a difficult word was far better than the constant vigilance and search for the easy way out. Through the years, I have found that this is still one of the best ways to reduce my anxiety and to improve my speech when I again begin to have trouble.

Being assertive means being aggressive. You don't need a therapist to harness this power. Search for those words or situations that are beginning to bug you rather than hiding them until they build up to giant fears. If you stutter on a particular word, you can deliberately use the word again in other conversations until the fear is gone. If a certain situation makes you tense so talking is difficult you can go back into similar situations until you feel more at ease. Where you used to avoid, search for positive constructive ways to reduce your fear and struggle. At times, it means bearing some temporary embarrassment while you stick it out on a hard word, but overall you'll find that your fear, tension, and struggle are less when you practice constructive assertiveness.

Exploring the Dreaded Unknown. Early in my therapy program, I made a startling discovery. Although I had stuttered for years, I really did not know much about what I did with my speech apparatus as I stuttered. Like many other persons who stutter, I had been so embarrassed when I was stuttering, that my total attention was drawn to trying to "get out of" my seemingly helpless struggle against an unexplainable "block." In therapy, my clinicians helped me learn to study my speech behaviors and to analyze what I was doing at those moments when I was struggling. Many of the things I was doing interfered with fluency more than they helped. Although in the past I'd repressed awareness of my stuttering behaviors, I now found that much was to be learned from encountering and analyzing them. You, too, can explore the unknown. When you do, you may find that you push your lips together too hard or jam your tongue against the roof of your mouth. You may notice that as you start to say a word, you build up too much tension.

> Many of the things I was doing interfered with fluency more than they helped.

Once you begin to see what you are doing that makes talking difficult, you find that much of this behavior is controllable. Concentrate on changing what you do when you stutter by doing differently some of the things that seem to interfere with your fluency. Stuttering will then lose some of its magical powers and become only those things which you do. Eventually you should make a very important discovery; that is, that you are not completely helpless at the moment you are stuttering.

Defining Realistic Obtainable Goals. Another helpful attribute that ties directly into the changes we've just been discussing

> You are not completely helpless at the moment you are stuttering.

is to set for yourself realistic and definable goals. Many of you will have, as I did, a rather perfectionistic attitude toward speaking. I wanted complete fluency with absolutely no stuttering. Anything less was a failure.

When you realize that all speakers have some hesitancy and disfluency in their speech, and when you realize that it is unrealistic to expect to change completely and immediately a problem you've lived with for years, you will be able to get satisfaction from small gains and to have greater tolerance for those difficulties you still encounter. Rather than hoping for complete fluency in each situation, work towards more realistic goals of improvement in certain specific behaviors, such as reduction of excessive lip tension.

Reducing the Importance of Stuttering. One of the hardest things for me to learn was that the problem of stuttering is not the worst thing that can happen. For years I had felt stuttering was the biggest problem in life and this affected my entire self-perception. I was definitely handicapped because I was a member of the small minority that stuttered. Getting older has many disadvantages, but it had the advantage of helping me put things in perspective. As I encountered other persons with other problems, I eventually realized that there are many difficulties worse than stuttering. One can still do most of what he wishes even if he does stutter.

Putting stuttering in a more realistic perspective may reduce some of your tension and make it easier for you to work on it. You should feel less embarrassed when it does occur, and you can stop thinking of yourself as a handicapped individual and thus improve your overall self-confidence.

Maintaining Improvements. Many of you who stutter have had the experience of getting better during therapy only to find yourself having trouble again when therapy is discontinued. This event, sometimes called a relapse, frequently leads to demoralization and the failure complex—a feeling that there's little use in trying to change your stuttering since it will probably return.

Frequently the person who has had this experience overacts to the return of struggle behaviors. He may well forget that even the amount of trouble he is having now is not nearly as frequent nor as severe as it was formerly. The fear of stuttering suddenly reappears and avoidance and struggle behaviors soon follow. Rather than accept this defeatist attitude, it's far better to go back to the basic principles; that is, determine what specific things you're doing and start again to do those things which you've found make talking easier.

Too many persons who stutter stop too soon after gaining some fluency and losing some of the fear. They fail to realize that stuttering behaviors have been learned on a complex reinforcement schedule over a long period of time. They fail to do those things which will maintain the new speaking behaviors. In all kinds of learning we normally go through three stages: (1) establishment of the new habit, (2) transfer of the habit to different situations, and (3) maintenance of the new behavior. If, after making some positive changes in your speech behavior, you revert to those attitudes and practices that originally were a part of the problem, you may find that the problem reappears.

To maintain the progress you've made in therapy it's wise to enlarge your speaking horizons. Now's the time to take that course in public speaking you've always dreaded or to begin to accept more invitations to social events where you know you'll have to meet a lot of people. Just as it's difficult to imagine maintaining recently learned swimming skills when you don't continue to go swimming, it seems pretty hard to imagine maintaining newly acquired attitudes and behaviors in speaking if you don't continue to enter a lot of speaking situations.

...enlarge your speaking horizons.

I hope some of my experiences will be helpful to you. Before ending, however, I must express a sincere debt of gratitude to the two persons who served as my clinicians some twenty-five years ago. They know who they are. I probably could have made many of the changes I've made without them, but I'm convinced they helped change my life for the better.

Chapter **15**

message to
adult stutterers

Gerald R. Moses

As a person who has stuttered for some time you have probably been more preoccupied and perplexed about this troublesome problem than any other aspect of your life. You have found that your stuttering interferes with and complicates even the most basic relationships with other people. Your expectations and hopes for personal, social and professional success have been limited by your feelings of being an inadequate talker.

You have found that concern for what others think of you has made you feel trapped and frustrated. You have wondered why you can talk freely in one situation and not at all in another. Most of all, you have asked, "Why Me? Why do I stutter and my friends do not?" You have tried to follow suggestions given by others. "Slow down, think what you are going to say, whistle, etc." You have even invented some of your own techniques for preventing the occurrence of stuttering. Most of these suggestions have had some foundation in distracting your attention from stuttering. Some of them have even worked for awhile. But temporary relief due to distraction has not solved your difficulties.

You have found much of what you have read and heard about stuttering to be confusing and embarrassing. While some writers feel that you stutter because you are physically different from people who do not stutter, others seem convinced that your stuttering lies in an emotional problem. Actually, persons who stutter seem to fall within the same range of physical and emotional characteristics as persons who do not stutter. The real difference between those who stutter and those who do not seems to be that stutterers stutter.

As the problem of stuttering develops, easy repetitions and prolongations are replaced by struggled attempts to say words. Embarrassment and the avoidance of words, situations and certain listeners occurs and a degree of emotionality is injected which complicates and compounds the problem. Penalty reactions by listeners convince you that your speech is unpleasant. This leads to further desperate attempts to prevent the occurrence of stuttering by whatever means available; struggle and avoidance are among the most commonly used.

During periods of crisis or conflict alternative ways to cope with and resolve problems present themselves. The range of alternatives is extreme. On the one hand we find flight or avoidance. On the other hand we find fight or struggle. Depending on the occasion either extreme might be appropriate, but a reasonable compromise seems to be more healthy, more effective and more generally used. When extreme measures become the rule the original problem has been compounded. On one hand, the problem becomes a struggle problem; on the other, an avoidance problem. The problem of stuttering develops or worsens when extreme reactions become learned as routine responses to what was once a more simple problem of speech disfluency.

Crucial to this point is the fact that struggle and avoidance *worsen* a problem of stuttering. Easy repetitions of sounds become hard repetitions with tension and facial contortion when force and hurry are added to them. Audiences react negatively to the struggle, and this convinced you that you must "try harder" so you increase your struggle. Similarly, penalty reactions to your stuttering prompt you to avoid or conceal your stuttering. Your speech becomes cautious and backward-moving. Your attention is directed to planning escape from stuttered words rather than to planning your thoughts. Avoidance strengthens your need to be fluent. The most evil part of this development is the subtle way in which struggle and avoidance become a part of you. They become involuntary and you do not recognize when you use them.

If you are serious about working to resolve your stuttering problem then it is time to change your approach to the problem.

Easy ways out of difficulty are momentarily convenient, but in the long run they reinforce the problem. Although a step-by-step approach to solving a problem of stuttering does not account for individual differences among those who stutter, the following suggestions are placed in the order of their importance.

> Easy ways out of difficulty in the long run reinforce the problem.

Reduce Avoidances. Determine to reduce your use of avoidances. Try to stutter openly and audibly. Let your stutterings be heard and seen rather than continue to conceal them by hurry and quiet. Try to keep your stuttering forward-moving and purposeful rather than postponed and half-hearted. Try to maintain eye contact with your listeners. Looking away severs the communication link with your audience and convinces them that you are ashamed and disgusted with the way that you talk. When you present yourself in an embarrassed and uncomfortable way you are more likely to receive negative audience reactions than if you stutter openly. Deliberately enter previously feared situations. Judge your performance on the basis of the degree to which you approached the situation rather than on the basis of how much you

> Deliberately enter previously feared situations.

stuttered or how fluent you were. Begin to recognize yourself as you are and as you want to be rather than as you think others want you to be. All of us need to be loved by, and in close contact with, other people. However, too much "human respect" makes us prisoners of what we think others want us to be.

Stutter in an Easier Way. When you are openly tackling the majority of your moments of stuttering you can try to change their form. Look at your stutterings objectively rather than emotionally. Study them by holding on to them longer than it would have taken to stutter-out the troublesome word. Resist the impulse to get the stuttering over with quickly. Although it is difficult to become less emotional about what you do, you need to become more realistic about yourself. For awhile, you must place greater emphasis on recognizing how you talk rather than on what others think of you.

Experiment with different ways to stutter for the purpose of learning how you stutter and the strength of your stuttering. Recognize and specify what you do when you stutter. Begin by listing the struggle behaviors that you use which are not a part of the act of speaking. Become aware of head or arm movements, eye blinking, other movements or body rigidity, lip-smacking or other noises, puffing of the cheeks or pursing of the lips. You will seek to eliminate these behaviors by increasing your awareness of them and separating them from your attempts to talk. Practice their use and insert them voluntarily into your speech when you have moments of less stuttering. Show yourself that they are not required for talking by using them independently of real and severe moments of stuttering.

Other behaviors which characterize your stuttering can be changed and normalized. Make an inventory of speech related struggle that accompanies your stuttering. Factors such as hurrying the utterance, tension in the lips, face and throat, and unusual preformations of sounds should be noted.

Normalize your attempts to say stuttered words. Normal speech is easy and forward-moving. Movements are released effortlessly. Try to prolong the first sound in a troublesome word until you feel you can release the rest of the word easily. If prolongations are uncomfortable for you, try an easy repetition of the first *syllable* of the word. Maintain the prolongation or repetition *out loud*. Make your approach to the word purposeful and straightforward. Your task is to learn to approach your stutterings openly and honestly and to eliminate the effort and hurry associated with previous attempts to talk. Judge your performance based on the degree of approach (stutter loud enough and long enough to examine what you are doing) and the degree of ease of release.

This is strong medicine! It is contrary to what you have improvised and learned. The emphasis is upon controlled *exhibition* of your stuttering, not upon inhibition. The number of times that you have previously inhibited your stuttering should suggest that many exhibitions will be needed to change significantly your manner of talking. Comfort in the use of normalized stuttering will follow only after much exercise. You may wish to select a friend or confidant with whom you can discuss your successes and failures, your heroics and flops. Your goal is not perfect speech, but rather the reduction of concern about your speech and the normalization of your attempts to talk.

Recognize and Tolerate Normal Disfluency. Normal speech contains disfluencies of many types. Easy repetitions of words and phrases, revisions, and incomplete phrases are a few types of normal disfluency. When these occur, and as long as they are *not* used as avoidance devices, they should be recognized as normal and not as symptoms of stuttering. Intolerance of normal disfluency causes you to try to talk with perfect fluency, an unattainable goal for anyone. Listen to these breaks in fluency in the speech of nonstuttering talkers. When the same kind of disfluencies occur in your own speech, they should be accepted and viewed as normal.

Again, these suggestions are strong medicine. I appreciate how difficult they seem. I encourage you to give them a fair trial. Finally, accept my best wishes for success and my respect for your determination to approach and resolve your problem of stuttering.

Chapter 16

some suggestions for gaining and sustaining improved fluency

David A. Daly

Like most individuals who stutter I went to bed each night praying that I would wake up fluent, and I awoke each day only to discover that my stuttering was still a reality. After several years of half-hearted attempts at speech therapy, I gave up on therapy and I gave up on my speech clinicians. Discouraged, despondent, and depressed I contemplated suicide, as well as becoming a monk in a religious order that required a vow of silence. I did neither. Instead, I limped along for a few years and somehow, by carefully selecting courses which required little or no oral participation, graduated from college. Feeling more comfortable in classes within the Speech-Language Pathology curriculum, I decided to pursue a master's degree in that field.

During my graduate training, two fluency clients I was assigned to treat complained to the program director that my stuttering was worse than theirs. After reassigning them to other clinicians, the director required me to see a speech-language pathologist myself. Surprisingly, this person listened when I discussed my dream of becoming perfectly fluent. (I had the illusion that perfectly fluent speech was possible.) This clinician did not argue or try to reason with me. Instead he said something like, "I don't know how fluent you might eventually become; why don't we work together and see?" He offered no promises. He gave no guarantees. But his patient yet confident manner persuaded me to give therapy one more try. His honest, reassuring, and sincere responses to my questions rekindled my hope for success which had been buried deep within me for so long. In retrospect, I suspect the bottom line which led to my significant improvement was that I trusted him. Below you will find some suggestions and guidelines for dealing with your stuttering which I hope will inspire and encourage you to pursue your quest to speak more fluently than you presently do. Improved fluency is possible!

You might be interested in knowing that I began this journey toward better speech during my mid-twenties when I was full of self-doubts. I was insecure, afraid of life, reluctant to try new things, and embarrassed about most things I did. Risk taking and trying new things were preceded by procrastination, dread, and fear of the future. I certainly was a challenge for any sincerely dedicated clinician.

Fortunately, this clinician helped me readjust my sights to more realistic, achievable goals. He convinced me that a more intelligent plan, rather than becoming perfectly fluent, might be to become as fluent as it was possible for me to become. Second, he helped me see that my stuttering was not a curse, but instead a challenge which I could devote time and effort to change. I set a goal to practice my fluency skills for at least five minutes a day.

> I needed to...readjust my sights to more realistic, achievable goals.

As I pushed myself to talk more and to practice the techniques my therapist taught, I discovered that small gains were possible if I attempted speech tasks that were simple, concrete, and doable. I began by putting 10 paperclips in my left front pocket each morning. Each time that I attempted and completed a specifically planned sentence, e.g., asking for directions to a certain store, I would move a paperclip to my right front pocket. At the end of the day I would count and write down how many clips I had moved. On days when I found only one or two clips in my right pocket, I mentally gave myself a kick in the seat of the pants. I was realizing that unless I made the effort to improve, progress would not be possible. Benjamin Franklin's words, "There can be no gain without pain" kept echoing in my mind. I vowed to try harder. Then I heard Yoda's words, "Do or do not, there is no try."

It is one thing to talk about assignments you are going to do but quite another thing to actually go out and do them. The more speech activities you do, the more progress you will see and the more control you have over your speech. And, by keeping a written account of the number of sentences planned and completed at the end of the week, visible verification of small gains is possible. Recognition of such efforts and small gains increase self confidence and put you closer to your eventual goal.

Speaking more, and becoming more comfortable doing it, have a powerful side benefits. They increase your self-esteem. Boosting your confidence makes you more willing to try even more challenging activities. Success breeds success. Like the turtle, people who stutter only make progress when they are willing to stick their necks out a little.

Prior to such success, I was afraid of change. I believed that my stuttering had kept me a "giant in chains." If only I didn't stutter, I reasoned, I could succeed at anything. Once in therapy, when asked to describe myself by listing some strengths and weaknesses on a large blackboard I wrote, "I stutter." Then I sat down. Slowly my clinician helped me see a larger picture of myself. And, he showed me that studying myself and my stuttering were productive, beneficial activities. I realized that instead of changing from who I was to something unknown, changing allowed me to become more of who I was.

As the various techniques suggested by your clinician and through the material you read yield more fluency (that is, less tense or choppy speech) some enthusiasm and desire to continue practicing may begin to wane or get lost. When this occurs, the older, more predictable stuttering patterns return. Leaving a comfort zone is never easy. Most human beings revert to what was accepted before. Furthermore, the newer fluency enhancing techniques which had become easy to do after diligent practice, also become easy *not* to do. Missing a day or two of practicing becomes more of a habit. What had become easy to do, then becomes easy not to do. Missed or inconsistent practicing almost always leads to a stuttering relapse. Successful clients adopt a simple motto: "Practicing a little every day helps the smoother, more fluent speech stay." I am reminded of the sage advice of Seneca who wrote: "Practice is the best of all instructors." Until your fluency skills are firmly established, incorporate some speech practice into your schedule each and every day.

> Practice is the best of all instructors.

Several research studies suggest that speech progress is not durable or lasting through behavioral speech methods alone. Along with regular speech practice, more and more clinicians and clients are reporting the benefits of simultaneously visualizing themselves speaking fluently. Olympic athletes and successful people from all walks of life have enthusiastically reported success by adding visualization exercises to their regular practice activities. In effect, success is achieved by pre-playing in the mind, as clearly and vividly as possible, scenes or images depicting the successful outcomes they desire. These are sound techniques which have worked for professional golfers and tennis players for years. I have witnessed the positive effect of incorporating similar visualization activities with myself and also with my clients who stutter.

Along with the traditional or fluency shaping therapy activities, you will need to take a few minutes to get relaxed: close your eyes, and visualize yourself speaking fluently in a variety of situations. One example might be making an introduction fluently. Repeated practice often allows you to see the scenes imagined more clearly. Olympic athletes contend that the clearer the picture imagined, the more likely it is to come true. Practice several different scenes, such as seeing yourself speaking smoothly on the telephone. This image, too, should be practiced again and again. Of course, other desired speaking situations are practiced. Repeated visualization practice is just as important as repeated oral speech practice.

Some researchers contend that these activities are based on self-fulfilling philosophy. That is, when a golfer tells himself that he won't make an easy putt, he often doesn't. When a baseball player says to himself, "I hope I don't strike out" he often does.

Similarly, when a person who stutters says, "I hope I don't stutter when answering the telephone," he often does. Under pressure, people tense up and often do exactly what they don't want to do. This certainly seems to be true for people who stutter. Visualize what you **do** want, not what you **do not** want. Be positive.

Visualization exercises enable fluency clients to see themselves, in their minds, speaking fluently without tension. Repeated practice at anything usually has a profound effect on future behavior. And, repeated practice increases a person's confidence that successful outcomes are possible. More fluent speech that is produced easily provides the evidence that such progress is possible.

Practicing positive visualizations has one major advantage over overt speech practice. It can be done silently, during times when speech practice is not possible. For example, visualization can be practiced while standing in line at a fast-food restaurant, waiting in a dentist or doctor's office, or riding in a car with others, etc. Several minutes may be captured from busy schedules by visualizing successful speaking activities while watching television. The commercial breaks are excellent short times to practice. We have found that "a little practice each day helps the fluency stay." Mary Wood, speaking at a self-help workshop, put it best I think. She said, "What we think about, we bring about."

In many ways life (and fluency) seems to be a self-fulfilling prophesy. Some people I have known believe that even doubling their amount of speech practice time, or adding visualization exercises to a therapy program, won't make any difference in their fluency. Research has shown that a person's belief and determination can make a definite difference.

Henry Ford said, "If you think you can or if you think you can't, you're probably right." One fact seems obvious: no matter how good specific treatment techniques or speech clinicians are, change only occurs when clients make a commitment to do the

If you think you can or if you think you can't, you're probably right.

work necessary for change. Practice is essential. Believing that positive changes in fluency are possible is important, too.

I believe combining speech and positive visualization activities is a useful, productive treatment regime that is helping scores of stuttering people who I know, and hundreds whom I don't know. What have you got to lose? You can practice successful speech outcomes in your mind several times a day without anyone knowing. It doesn't cost anything, and maybe you will find your attitude changing a little. Maybe you will believe in the possibility of your eventual progress even more. You might even see some benefits and positive results.

If what you've been doing in the past isn't working, why not give *concentrated, focused speech practice* and *visualization exercises* a try. You know for sure that if you don't do something, nothing is going to change.

What have you got to lose?

Chapter 17

change: potential qualities become actualities

Joseph G. Agnello

I had a severe stuttering problem until the age of 28. What brought on some of the miraculous changes in my speech can be attributed to my therapist, Dr. Charles Van Riper (Van), and my efforts to meet the challenges he presented.

Therapy with Van brought about a more dramatic change in my attitude than in my speech performance. When therapy was terminated, I was satisfied with my progress even though I still had repetitions and blocks. I had earned my master's degrees and was headed to The Ohio State University for doctoral work with Dr. John W. Black, the one person Van trusted to preserve the gains I had made in therapy. Most satisfying, however, was that I felt I could move forward in my speech. For the first time in my life, I was free to express all kinds of thoughts. There was minimal avoidance of sounds, words, people and situations. I could order a strawberry soda without being traumatized. For me, this was as good as being 'cured.' I had discovered that every act of speech could be a challenge that need not end in failure. "Learn from failure... don't perpetuate failure." These are among Van's challenges that I try to convey in this chapter.

Prior to therapy, I had many false notions about why I stuttered. People gave advice, yet none of it appeared to do much good. I felt stuttering was an unresolvable condition. In all fairness, some of the advice I received was good; I simply didn't understand it, was not ready to make use of it and, consequently, rejected it. Advice that one cannot act upon to bring about change is usually discarded; in many respects, this is unfortunate.

People who stutter often harbor negative thoughts about speech, themselves, and others. These thoughts only perpetuate the problem, and prevent the person from identifying and acting on good advice. Furthermore, these thoughts have little validity. During my early years, I was plagued with negative thoughts: I can't talk; I stutter because there is something wrong with my mind; I'm mentally slow; I have a nervous condition; my father is mean and embarrassed about my stuttering; I think faster than I talk. Fluency, I thought, was due to positive traits and feelings: I'm a good athlete; I have a good sense of humor; I feel relaxed; I'm not thinking about stuttering. Finally, there were the 'whys': Why do I stutter?; Why am I sometimes fluent?; WHY? To dwell on such thoughts and questions only perpetuates the idea of having a 'condition.' When I thought I had a condition, I believed the solution to stuttering was simply not to stutter. It was a shock to realize I had a problem; the tremendous task of solving this problem was daunting.

An episode with Van illustrates this idea of stuttering as a problem, not a condition. This event was instrumental in motivating me to work on my attitude and speech skills and drove the remarkable changes in my character and speech during the years of therapy and beyond.

I was in the midst of therapy and much discussion focused on "fake stuttering." This was simply to do, consciously and deliberately, what I had always tried not to do: stutter. To fake stutter was a challenge I couldn't meet, and I became depressed over my lack of progress.

One day, Van asked that I accompany him to Allegan, Michigan, for his breakfast speech to the Lion's Club. Van picked me up at 6:00 a.m. the following morning. I had been up most of the night worrying that I would have to speak and never bothered to shower or shave. I was dying for a cup of coffee and a donut when Van pulled up to a little diner on U.S. 131. Inside, a few truckers sat laughing and talking at a table. Van and I sat down at the counter. The waiter approached and asked for my order.

I began to stutter. I looked down at the counter; all I could see was the waiter's greasy apron stretched over his huge belly. I was sure he was amused by my distress. With my left hand wrapped around my head and my mouth contorted, I continued to struggle over the first syllable of my order. I became more aware of the truckers' laughter—obviously over my predicament. I finally forced out "c-c-c-coffee" and decided to forget about the donut. The waiter turned to Van for his order; I was off the hook! Relief turned to amazement as I heard Van begin to fake stutter.

I was shocked by the waiter's expression as Van stuttered through his order of coffee and donuts for both of us; it was so pleasant. I peeked at the truckers. They were still talking and laughing, but completely oblivious to our presence. The waiter said in a matter-of-fact tone, "Never had two of you guys with stuttering. My brother stutters." Van replied, "Yes, we both s-s-s-stutter. I am a professor, and my friend and I are g-g-going to Allegan to give a b-b-b-breakfast speech." The waiter said, "That's great!"—and turned to fill Van's order. What I observed while Van was stuttering was totally contrary to what I believed had occurred while I was ordering.

During the following week, I was dejected by how wrong I had been through the years in thinking that my stuttering was due to others' reactions. I was eager to discuss this with Van. When I came to him, I was in tears. I said, "My problem isn't stuttering, is it?" Van took a long pause, gave an affirmative shake of his head, and replied, "Now we can begin work!"

Now we can begin work!

It was this discovery of false notions that helped me to gain further insight into my problem and learn to manage my speech. I began to question myself: Is part of my problem not knowing

90

how to relate to people? What do people think about my stuttering? Do they really care that I stutter? Does the way I react to my stuttering determine how others react? Do I listen to others? How do others talk and listen? What beliefs and ideas stand in my way of progress? Should I try to "stutter easily" as Van suggested? As I accepted Van's challenges, I no longer felt bound to my old pattern of stuttering. I could move forward and plan my own course of action. I stopped avoiding speech. Stuttering no longer controlled me.

Most people are gentle, well meaning, and generally interested in what others have to say. The fact that you stutter has little to do with what others think of you. Speech is a social process: a public affair. As part of society, you have a responsibility to communicate with others, but remember, establishing good relationships through verbal exchanges is a learned skill. Organize your discourse. Think clearly of what you want to say and how to say it. Speak in a clear and forthright manner, and monitor your delivery: Should I speak slower and initiate speech more easily? Should I pause more frequently? Finally, think critically about your listeners: What information and experience do they bring to the exchange? Am I afraid of her, or she of me? How can I help him understand what I say? People may respond in a way you never imagined!

As a speech scientist and therapist, I have spent many hours observing others with fluency problems and performed acoustic and physiologic analyses of 'how stutterers stutter.' This has forced me to critically examine my own speech and the ways in which I approach certain words and move from one syllable to the next. My observations and experiments have led me to identify a universal feature of stuttered speech: *timing problems.*

Proper timing is crucial to forward-moving speech. Voicing begins and ends many times during speech and must be coordinated precisely with other articulatory gestures. Movement of the vocal cords excites air in the throat and mouth (producing sound)

Proper timing is crucial to forward-moving speech

and other articulatory gestures such as movement of the tongue, lips, and jaw, modify that sound (producing speech.) Any articulatory actions that involve an 'easy onset' (smooth initiation of a sound) or a smooth transition from sound to sound will facilitate forward-moving speech.

Beyond the matter of timing is another form of stuttering that I believe to be prevalent, but not as obvious: stuttering during the process of organizing thoughts, or becoming fixed on the notion that "I can't say that sound" during an episode of stuttering. Thoughts are organized in phrases, and one phrase must flow smoothly to another. Any effort that disrupts, discourages, or fails to assist a smooth transition from phrase to phrase will promote the breakdown of forward-moving speech. The breakdown may not only be characterized by stuttering, but also by lack of focus on ideas and reasons for engaging in speech communication. The focus becomes the stuttering itself: the sounds, postures, and helpless notion that "I can't say it." You must realize this is not a valid attitude. You can learn to speak in a forward-moving manner.

The following practices have helped in my efforts to improve my speech:

- Speak in the style of a good orator. Carl Sandburg spoke slowly, prolonging vowels and pauses. He was my model.

- Stutter deliberately (fake stutter) with at least one objective in mind, such as maintaining eye contact. By doing so, you assume responsibility for yourself and your listener. Test your reactions and the reactions of your listeners. If the fake stutter becomes 'real,' or if you fail to be objective and critical about your stuttering, you are probably responding to false assumptions. What are they? Is your stuttering real when you are out of control? You must try again and seek a small measure of success on one objective.

- Speak slowly and deliberately. Stutter slowly and deliberately. Experiment with easy onsets and 'loose pullouts' (smooth releases of sounds), especially if you become stuck. Efficient and intelligible speech involves minimal physical effort. Thinking that you must force or struggle is a belief to overcome by accumulating small successes.

- Listen to and/or watch audio and videotaped recordings of yourself in speech situations.

- Speak honestly with others, especially family and friends, about your stuttering. Discuss how you perceive yourself and others, and how you think others perceive you.

The following developments were instrumental in acquiring what I consider to be good communication skills:

- Giving up efforts to explain my stuttering to myself.

- Organizing what I wished to say, and the manner in which I wished to say it. This enabled me to move forward in my speech even if I stuttered.

- Answering pertinent questions about myself and my speech through serious introspection and self-confrontation.

- Assuming responsibility for talking, and regarding others with whom I was speaking. Part of this was listening attentively without distraction.

- Learning to reserve judgments about myself and others.

- Learning the value of pauses during speech communication.

It is difficult to work on attitudes, beliefs, and speech skills. However, if you are consistent in your practice—alone and in speaking situations—speech will become easier. Experimenting will become fun. You may need the help of a friend, speech therapist, and/or support group. Consider exploring the Internet for sites pertaining to stuttering.

In your efforts, try to move from Column A to Column B.

	A: REACTIVE		B: PROACTIVE
1.	Fear of speaking.	1.	Seeking speech situations for discovery.
2.	Fear of rejection.	2.	Assuming responsibility for talking. (Approval comes from the content of your speech, not from fluency.)
3.	Fear of failure.	3.	Fascination with outcome. Learn from failure.
4.	Aversion to risk.	4.	Taking chances with slow, deliberate speech, easy onsets, loose pullouts, and fake stuttering. (Possibilities are infinite!)
5.	Compulsive effort for perfection.	5.	Looking beyond exact techniques for perfect control; increasing tolerance for error; appreciating your efforts and progress.
6.	Judging self and others.	6.	Observing self and others.

Best of luck to you as you move forward.

Chapter **18**

four steps to freedom

Richard M. Boehmler

I have found that those who have obtained freedom from their stuttering successfully solved four basic problems:

a. **Identifying** the specific nature of their stuttering,

b. **Developing** an effective therapy program,

c. **Implementing** that therapy program, and

d. **Maintaining** the new speech production patterns until they became habitual.

But first, a word of caution before examining these steps in detail. Stuttering can vary significantly from one individual to another. Therefore, some of the following generalizations may not apply to all stuttering patterns.

Identification

Knowing that you "stutter" is not enough. Your unique stuttering needs to be identified. Self-diagnosis is a difficult task. Put your best effort into this step.

Start by describing exactly what you do or do not do when you wish to speak and stuttering occurs. Speech production involves the integration and timing of two major processes: (1) **language formulation** (the thought process of putting ideas into words) and (2) **vocal output** (the phonation/ voicing process of making sounds with your vocal chords, and the articulation process of making sounds using the lips and tongue and modifying sounds made by phonation.) This integration occurs in short sequences called utterances. An utterance is produced as a continuous sequence of movements without a pause. These movements occur so fast that you often start the movements for one sound before the movements for the previous sound has been completed. Utterances vary in length from one to many syllables. For example, the utterance "I want to go home" could be said as:

one utterance without a pause,   "iwanttogohome"

two utterances, with a pause after "I"   "I wanttogohome"

five utterances with a pause after   "I, want, to, go, home."
each word for emphasis

These units of speech are usually produced automatically with near-perfect precision, but errors do occur which may stop the normal flow of speech.

Examine utterances in which your stuttering occurs and describe the specific movements, feelings, or actions which characterize that stuttering. If the speech mechanism is blocked, describe exactly which muscles do not move in the appropriate fashion and what you do about the block. For example: my tongue did not move back from behind my teeth to produce the "t" sound; I held my breath which stopped the air flow needed to produce "h"; when I anticipated a block, I either substituted another word or articulated the word with more effort to override the block. Making a video recording or asking a friend for feedback may help. I have found it useful to divide these observations into three categories: (1) speech-flow blocks, (2) block-coping patterns and (3) patterns not associated with blocks.

1. Speech-flow blocks:

Blocks are breaks in the flow of speech which are unintentional and undesired. Speech-flow blocks can occur for numerous reasons. For example: we can have problems with language formulation due to problems remembering a common name or term. Or, we can have difficulty because the brain's motor command to the speech muscles is not properly timed and results in movements that are not properly sequenced. A third type of problem occurs when the rate of movement for a complex pattern exceeds the ability of our muscles to execute that command. A fourth reason could be when an emotional response (anxiety) interferes with our ability to properly use the speech production mechanism because anxiety can cause the vocal chords and breathing mechanism to respond in ways which are incompatible with smooth speech production. Finally, various other breathing, voicing/phonation, and articulatory patterns such as trying to continue speech-flow when most of the air has been exhaled from the lungs, can contribute to speech-flow stoppages.

The block alone occupies only a small fraction of a second. As soon as a block is perceived, the speaker copes by doing something to initiate or maintain speech-flow. When identifying your stuttering, try to distinguish between blocks and block-coping patterns.

2. Block-coping patterns:

Most individuals learn effective block-coping patterns. However, some of us use patterns which make matters worse by perpetuating the cause of the blocks or by adding undesired behaviors. In many cases these ineffective block-coping patterns make up most of our stuttering. They include such responses as "pushing" to complete the word, adding a movement such as a head jerk to "release" a block, or substituting another word to avoid an anticipated block.

3. Patterns not associated with blocks:

Some stuttering patterns are not perceived by the speaker as a block, nor are they behaviors to cope with the expectation or occurrence of a block. For example, if the rate of vocal output exceeds the rate of language formulation, extra syllables which have previously been formulated may be automatically produced in order to keep the rhythm of vocal output going. If one has the idea "I want to go home" and starts vocal output after formulating "I" but proceeds at a rate too fast for formulating the complete sentence, the result may be "I - I - I want to go home." Note that such an idea would usually be produced as one utterance without a break in the movement pattern. The repetition of "I" may not be noticed by either the speaker or listener and no stoppage or block of speech-flow would occur. However, when such repetitions are frequent they might be noticed by the listener and be perceived as stuttering.

After identifying your block, block-coping, and non-block associated stuttering patterns, you need to decide what patterns you wish to reduce or eliminate. This decision or goal becomes the basis for designing a self-therapy program.

Developing an Effective Therapy Program.

The speech production patterns of others can be used as the model for designing a therapy program. The speech of most normally fluent speakers contains a number of characteristics which are important for understanding why you stutter and what skills you need to achieve free-flowing production. It has been my observation that: (1) some blocks in speech-flow are to be expected in normal production, but blocks due to speech-flow anxiety are rare; (2) coping with blocks without increased muscle effort in a smooth efficient manner, and without increasing the likelihood of more blocks, seem to be a common skill; (3) confidence in one's ability to initiate and maintain speech-flow is typical; (4) the integration of vocal output and language formulation is such that the rate of vocal output is continuously adjusted to match the varying rate of language formulation and the complexity of the muscle sequence of that utterance; (5) most speakers maintain a cushion between their fastest articulation rates and the limits of their speech production skills; and (6) the articulation rates of utterances in syllables-per-second varies significantly, with one's fastest utterances often three times as fast as one's slowest utterances.

Normal speech production is a very complex process requiring exceedingly fine muscle movements and the close integration of those movements and language formulation. Errors, including blocks, are to be expected. Even the less complex patterns involved in typing or playing golf are not executed perfectly every time. Therefore, effective block-coping is often the most critical skill for initiating and maintaining free-flowing speech. This is particularly true when a significant portion of one's stuttering behavior represents ineffective block-coping. You may need to develop the skill of coping with blocks without avoidance, increased effort, or added extraneous movements as the first step in your therapy program, with reduction of blocks and stuttering patterns not associated with blocks as second or third steps.

1. Effective block-coping skills:

A very common block coping strategy used by normal speakers when anticipating or experiencing a block is to instantaneously reduce the rate of speech movement and execute that movement with greater conscious control than is normally needed for automatic production. This change in articulatory rate over the production of one or two sounds/syllables is done without a pause or stopping the flow of the utterance. Practice counting from one to six as one continuous movement sequence Then repeat the sequence while significantly slowing the rate of movement on just one number without pausing. Practice doing this while reading out loud, randomly selecting various specific movements within each utterance on which to significantly slow down. When you can do this smoothly without a pause, try applying this control when expecting or experiencing a block in speech-flow.

2. Block reduction:

In some cases the high frequency of speech-flow blocks needs direct attention. In such cases, therapy needs to focus on factors which cause their occurrence. If anxiety is one of the causes, developing an effective block-coping skill to the point that it is applied with confidence may provide a foundation for reducing that anxiety. Other anxiety reducing techniques are also available and discussed by other authors in this publication. Frequent blocks, due to the complexity of the muscle sequence or language formulation difficulties, suggest the need to change the habitual range of one's articulation rate either by lowering the entire rate range or reducing the rate range by eliminating the fastest rates. There should be a cushion between the fastest articulatory rates and the rate that speech-flow breakdowns begin to occur. Sometimes incorrect breathing, phonation, or articulatory patterns may need attention.

3. Stuttering patterns not associated with blocks:

In most cases stuttering patterns not associated with blocks, such as simple, relaxed syllable repetitions, can be eliminated or reduced by establishing an articulatory rate range which provides more cushion between your fastest rate and the limits of your language formulation/vocal output integration system. I have found this to be a critical therapy component when the individual with frequent, simple syllable repetitions also needs to slide over some sounds in order to maintain their rate of syllable production.

Implementing a Therapy Program.

Stuttering therapy is work! You can't expect to establish new speaking patterns without a significant amount of effort. My best advice is to "plan your work and work your plan." Specific daily goals, procedures to reach those goals, and evaluation of your progress should be the norm. A few days without progress suggests a need to revise your problem description, therapy plan, or implementation program.

Maintenance

Normal speech is usually an automatic process. Any skills you have developed for achieving free-flowing speech must be maintained until you use those skills with little or no awareness or effort. They must become part of your speech production habit system to replace your stuttering habit system.

It is very common for individuals to start self-therapy with a high level of motivation. Careful identification, good therapy planning, and consistent implementation often leads to significant improvement. With that improvement, motivation to work hard at therapy often goes down. There is a strong tendency to let the "little stutters" go by since the listener "probably doesn't notice them." Planning is put off and implementation becomes inconsistent. A relapse to old stuttering patterns is likely to follow. The old stuttering habits have not disappeared. Motivation must be kept high until the new skills are habitual and consistently replace the stuttering habits.

Freedom to initiate and maintain speech-flow is possible. To achieve this freedom, I advise you to work on these four basic steps: **identify, plan, work, then follow-through!**

Chapter **19**

recovery journal

Bill Murphy

This year I celebrate my fiftieth birthday—a half century—and it has been a time for reflection. My life has been a roller coaster of both good and bad experiences. Looking back, one issue clearly stands out: my stuttering. Although my parents told me I stuttered as a preschooler, my personal recollections don't begin until third grade. My teacher asked each of us to share with the class what we had done over the summer break. I remember cutting short my description of a Cub Scout camping trip because the words seemed to be catching in my mouth and throat. At that moment I believe my journey for smoother speech began, and what a journey it has been. Certainly an adventure, sometimes full of hope and periods of success, but also of failure, especially in the early years. At times the stuttering seemed as hideous as the monsters I so feared in the childhood movies I watched. The journey has taken me down numerous roads, many leading to dead ends. I've also grown in innumerable ways and achieved things I never dreamed possible.

Hindsight is not always accurate; it is often colored by fuzzy memories. But looking back, I believe my stuttering elicited at least three distinct feelings. In those days I didn't possess the knowledge or maturity to fully understand these emotions. Today it's much easier. Today, I recognize one of the first feelings I experienced was *anxiety*. Stuttering quickly became something to dread. Not just the fear of being unable to say certain words, but other possible consequences of stuttering. People may ridicule me, not want to be my friend. There were fears of acting in a play, asking for candy at the store or making phone calls. Could I get a job or say my marriage vows? The second feeling was *shame*. I now know shame is an emotion that comes from believing that one is basically flawed. It seemed a part of me was defective and must be hidden at all costs. And, there was *guilt*. After all, I knew I didn't stutter all the time. Since at times I was speaking correctly, it followed that when I stuttered, I must be doing something wrong. If I could only speak fluently, all would be okay. Yet no matter how hard I tried, the stuttering was still present. The best I could manage was to engage in tricks to hide the stuttering. All kinds of weird avoidance behaviors were tried: changing words, talking around and around a topic but never saying directly what I meant because I would have stuttered. I tapped my fingers while talking and danced a little jig. I told people my name was Frank or Phil because these names contained easy sounds. I pretended to cough or told the teacher I didn't know the answers. I was a fake—a dishonest person.

The next twelve or so years were spent trying not to stutter, creating elaborate disguises, always looking for ways to hide the "secret" that most people eventually discovered. For brevity, I'll simply describe my childhood and adolescent years as being difficult. My family, friends, teachers and the few speech language pathologists I saw simply did not understand stuttering and their responses only aggravated the disorder. Stuttering was not helped by my family's membership in the Catholic church. Although the priests and nuns wanted to comfort me, they were of little help. I was repeatedly told to say Acts of Contrition for my sins and that prayer would lead God to heal even the worst sinner. Although I was never quite sure how my stuttering fit into this religious paradigm, I assumed that I must be bad or unworthy. In spite of these events, I believe my family, friends, and teachers cared for me and did the best they could. In retrospect, that's all one can ask for.

The university provided my first true successes. Several kind professors attempted to help by introducing a mixture of treatment approaches, including rate reduction, breath control, relaxation, and later in graduate school, employing time out from talking as part of an operant conditioning program. These approaches helped me to attain a little more fluency. At the time this was beneficial because I still believed success was measured only be the degree of fluency one attained. Unfortunately when the old stuttering monster reared its ugly head I could do nothing more than struggle, all the while feeling more shame, guilt, and anxiety. I began to read the works of Charles Van Riper who gave his clients incredible assignments such as stuttering on purpose and other fear reducing tasks. His methods were

Bring the stuttering out in the open.

different from any other person, and I secretly wished he were my therapist. Although my professors did not seem to understand stuttering as did Van Riper, I am still thankful for their help. They were kind and supportive. Most of all they helped me to bring the stuttering out in the open, to examine the phenomenon in a less emotional, more scientific manner.

Of particular impact was a psychology professor, who himself had a physical disability. This dear man coaxed me to address the class regarding my stuttering. Anxiety was high and although I don't recall a word I said, I had my first exposure to the act of self disclosure. I told the audience that I stuttered. After this experience it was easier to talk in class and the more I spoke openly, the better I felt. Although I quickly discarded this openness when the class ended, I believe this was the first step in my recovery. I didn't know it at the time, but my journey was now on the right road. I decided to become a speech pathologist and to spend time helping myself and others.

Following graduation I held several positions as a speech pathologist, all the while continuing my quest for fluency by still attempting to inhibit the occurrence of stuttering. The horizon for controlling stuttering looked bright. A new therapy called "fluency shaping" was beginning to take hold. I jumped on board with both feet, trying to control my stuttering through the techniques called airflow, continuous voicing, and easy onsets. I joined the staff at Purdue University. Here I met Peter Ramig who was working on his Ph.D. Peter, a stutterer himself, had worked with Lois Nelson who had, herself, been a client of Charles Van Riper. My love affair with Van Riper was rekindled. I had my first good look at stuttering modification. Peter and I continued the struggle to change our stuttering. Together we attempted cancellations, pullouts, and preparatory sets. And again I made progress, but deep inside my goal was to become a normal speaker.

On the heels of this experience, came the most significant milepost in my recovery journey. I was able to work with Joseph Sheehan. Sheehan asked me to consider a series of questions. "Was my progress using avoidance behaviors and attempts to directly stop stuttering really that successful both in the amount of fluency and emotional relief? What would happen if I tried to fully accept myself as someone who stuttered? What would happen if I allowed myself to stutter purposely, but in a new or easier manner, without the pretext of being a normal speaker?"

These questions both excited and frightened me. I began to use Sheehan's voluntary stuttering, which consists of prolonging, or "sliding," on the first sound of nonstuttered words. It was a means to advertise stuttering, to get the secret into the open, to desensitize. As voluntary stuttering increased, real stuttering decreased. This was not magic: stuttering usually decreases when speech patterns are altered and fluency increases. But there was a difference. Fluency was elicited not through avoidance or attempts to hide stuttering, but by acknowledging the disorder and purposefully doing what was feared.

Slowly and painfully a new self-image formed, which included accepting and embracing the role of a stutterer. Success began to be defined, not in terms of being a fluent speaker, but rather as a "good stutterer." Could I not become the "best possible stutterer?" It certainly wasn't the proverbial light switching on, but perhaps a slow twist of the rheostat. The road to recovery became clearer. I forced myself to talk to friends about stuttering and learned it was not so much the actual stuttering that bothered them, but rather the evident embarrassment, anxiety and inability to

> The secret was out and I was less tense and fearful.

discuss stuttering openly. After much trial and error I became proficient discussing disfluencies in appropriate social discourse. When I openly shared my stuttering, this put most listeners at ease. They asked questions about stuttering; people were interested, not revolted. When I chose to self-disclose stuttering, the secret was out and I was less tense and fearful. The more stuttering was discussed, the less shame, guilt, and anxiety were experienced. Voluntary exposure quiets these emotions.

It was time to tackle the stuttering that remained, and Sheehan's advice was helpful. I tried to overlay the sound stretching behavior used in voluntary stuttering on top of a true stuttering moment, at the same time adding missing speech components such as voicing. The goal was to let go of the need to stop or control the stutter, and manage it through a shaping process. Realizing that the fear of stuttering remained strong I attempted to accelerate the desensitization process by using Van Riper's pseudo-stuttering. These were not the smooth, voluntary "slides" associated with Joe Sheehan, but rather the purposeful imitations of real stuttering. This is an exceptionally difficult task but when done repetitively, it has significant fear reducing properties.

Old, bad feelings of past attempts to disguise stuttering continued to revisit me. To lessen the effects of these ghosts, I began to write shame stories. Shame stories recounted old, crazy, and inappropriate actions I had used to try to hide stuttering. Writing these stories were cathartic, especially when shared with my wife, and later with friends. The stories were well received; some were published in a support group newsletter. Continuing my attempts at self disclosure and desensitization, I began to sign letters to friends, B-B-Bill. This so delighted the two young children of friends that they gave me a present of hundreds of pencils, stamped on the side with "B-B-Bill." I still hand these out today.

I also made peace with my old nemesis, Porky Pig. Attending movies with my friends, I would feel like crawling under the seat when Porky Pig came on the screen. Today, Porky provides me with a wonderful way to continue my desensitization and self-disclosure. Thanks to my wife's gifts, I frequently wear my Porky Pig pin or take my Porky Pig coffee cup whenever I attend meetings and meet new people. These conversation starters that help serve as "shame-busters."

Perhaps a major point to be made from these exercises is that stuttering involves a symbiotic relationship between speaker and listener. This relationship can be negative or positive. I chose to make it positive. If I'm able to provide the listener with a degree of comfort regarding stuttering, then I'm more comfortable, have less disfluencies and better manage the remaining stuttering.

In summary, I had to accept the problem as my own. It was important to acknowledge that stuttering was not going to magically disappear. Running from or avoiding stuttering was not the way out. Recognition and reconciliation as a person who stutters was mandatory. Recovery meant studying stuttering patterns. What did I do when I stuttered, e.g., close my eyes, nod my head etc.? Allowing speech pattern changes, accepting less than perfect speech—a middle ground between hard stuttering and fluent speech was necessary. Attempts to control, prevent, eliminate stuttering, sent me backwards. Acknowledging, accepting, embracing stuttering pushed me forward, further and further into recovery. I can now talk to store clerks, use the telephone, give lectures and converse easily with friends, colleagues, and strangers. Do I still sometimes stutter? Of course I do. Do I sometimes experience a little shame and anxiety? Sure, it still happens. But I know how to manage the feelings and my speech.

I've been lucky. I've been privileged to take this recovery journey with tremendous love and support. I have the best family one could ask for. Many friends, both those who stutter and ones that don't, have given me security and love. We all have our adversaries in life. No one escapes. I suppose it's trite to say that life is a journey. But certainly it is. In many ways it's a spiritual journey, trying to find answers to the many questions we all have. Who are we, what are we here for and what can we do best? This is very serious stuff. On the other hand I have to remember not to take myself too seriously. It's best to have a sense of humor.

So in ending, I would like to quote a famous personality. As Porky Pig has been known to say, "Th-Th-Th- ah—that's all folks!"

face your fears

Sol Adler

My youth, as is the case with so many stutterers, was filled with alternate hope and despair as I hungered for some relief from my stuttering. This of course is not unique; most stutterers have had similar feelings. But have you ever asked yourself what it is that really bothers you, what it is that causes despair? Is it your stuttering or is it your fear of people's reactions to your stuttering? Isn't it the latter? Most stutterers have too much anxiety about what they think people might say or might do as a result of the stuttering. These anxieties can be lessened.

I remember well these feelings of worry, anxiety, and despair. If you can learn to dissipate some of these terrible feelings—you will be able to help yourself as many other stutterers have done.

There is one effective method you can utilize to achieve this goal. Face your fears! This advice is easy to give and admittedly difficult for many of you to take; however, it is advice that has helped many stutterers and it can help you.

Learn to face your fears of stuttering in different speech situations. My involvement in such "situational-work" during my early career created peace of mind for me. It was a slow process; I didn't achieve such freedom all in one day or week or month; and it was hard work. But I did it, and others have done it, and so can you.

Somehow you must learn to desensitize yourself to the reactions of others and refuse to let people's actual or imagined responses to your stuttering continue to affect your mental health or your peace of mind.

This is easier said than done but it can be accomplished. I found that by facing my fears

Desensitize yourself to the reactions of others.

gradually I was able to achieve such a goal, and I have known other stutterers who have "thrown" themselves into similar confrontations. Use whatever pace that best suits you, but get involved, one way or another, in these confrontations with your "speech fears." There will be times when you will be unable to face the fears inherent in different situations, but persevere. Don't give up! Continue facing your fears as often as you can. Besides the peace of mind that develops, you will also become more fluent in your speech. You will find yourself manifesting lesser amounts of stuttering and that stuttering will never be as severe as it was previous to your confrontation.

You will find that as you grow older you will develop more ability to do these things. With growing maturity we can generally face our fears more frequently and more consistently. But how long do you want to wait?

List all the speech situations in which you fear stuttering. These are pretty standard situations; for example, most stutterers fear using the telephone. They experience much distress when they are called upon to answer the telephone while it rings incessantly, or conversely, when they must place a necessary call. I remember well how often I "played-deaf" when the telephone would ring. Sometimes, unfortunately, I might be standing and more than a few feet from that ringing telephone, and my protestations regarding "answer what telephone?" would be of no avail. Face this fear by making many telephone calls each day to different persons—people whose names are unknown to you. Practice stuttering while you speak to them. Stutter in different ways. For example, I once had a patient make such a call and the party on the other end turned out to be a preacher. The patient had been told he must ask for J-J-J-J but to never complete the name. The preacher was an extraordinarily kind person and evidently with some time to spare. He continually urged the patient to "take it easy" and assured him that he wouldn't hang up. For two or three minutes the patient continued repeating the initial "J" until, in sheer desperation, the preacher said, "Son, there is no "J" here. I'm sorry but I have to go," and with that he hung up.

What do stutterers learn from this and similar experiences? Not to be as afraid of answering the telephone since the worst possible thing that could happen to him would be for the party to hang up on him, or to say something derogatory to him. In either case, his world doesn't end. By such experiences you will find yourself getting toughened caring less about how people might respond to you and, finally, you will be able to use the phone with lesser amounts of fear, anxiety, and stuttering.

Another classic situation most stutterers fear is asking questions of strangers. I suspect that this bothers you too. What I did, and have my patients do, is to stop people who are walking somewhere, or are in stores, and ask them questions concerning the time, directions, the price of some object, etc. All student clinicians who have trained under my supervision have been asked *to do first whatever* they ask the patient to accomplish. Thus they too had to first ask such questions of strangers. But since they were not stutterers, they had to feign stuttering and they were required to do it very convincingly.

These normal speakers discovered, as you well known, that much anxiety is experienced when asked to perform as indicated. But anxiety becomes reduced and dissipated if you engage in these kinds of situational experiences rapidly, one after another, almost without pause. For example: ask ten or fifteen people about their views regarding the cause of stuttering. You will find that after the eighth or ninth person has responded you will no longer possess all the fears you did when you initiated this exercise. Also, as a bonus, you might be surprised to find yourself actually listening to and arguing with your respondents and actually enjoying the exercise.

To argue about and/or to discuss effectively with anyone the causes or nature of stuttering means that you have to have some relevant information about stuttering. Do you know what this speech disorder is all about? If not, you should. You should learn as much about it as is possible. If your library does not contain sufficient information, write to the publisher of this book for additional information. No longer tolerate the false information from your parents, friends, teachers or others who are interested in you, and want to help, but who are probably very ignorant about stuttering. Educate them! But educate yourself first!

I discovered also that by talking to other stutterers I received indirectly the benefits of their therapeutic experiences. Find other stutterers! It may surprise you to find out how many fellow stutterers are available. Form groups! In this way you can help each other. It will be so much easier for you when you can find someone in whom you can confide and who understands your problem. Work up your own situational assignments. Alternate as clinician and patient with the proviso that the "clinician" must first do whatever he asks the "patient" to do. Watch people closely! See how they react to your stuttering. Do you see facial grimaces or indications of shock or surprise on their faces? Occasionally you may but often you may not. You will find that when you both become objective enough to observe these people carefully, and to compare notes regarding their responses, you may even begin to enjoy the exercise. Your group should also try to obtain the services of a competent and sympathetic professional person who can guide you in discussions regarding those factors involving personality development. If not, discuss them yourselves. This kind of introspection—or self-analysis— helped me a great deal. It made me look at myself to see what made me tick. I began to realize that much of the behavior I disliked in myself was motivated by my fear of stuttering.

In summary I have suggested two matters of great importance to you regarding your stuttering: (1) Learn all about stuttering; read everything you can regarding this disorder; there is much literature available. (2) Face your fears as often and as consistently as you can. Do not give up if and when you backtrack; try to meet "head-on" these feared situations. When you can do so with some degree of consistency, you may find a new life awaiting you.

Chapter 21

attacking the iceberg of stuttering: icepicks, axes, and sunshine!

Larry Molt

Years ago the late Joseph Sheehan, (see chapter 6) compared stuttering to an iceberg. The stuttering behaviors we see at the surface, above the water (the repetitions, blocks, substituted words, physical struggle) are just the tip of the iceberg. The greatest portions of what maintains stuttering lurks unseen in the depths. Four decades later this remains a fit analogy. My own experience as a person who stutters, speech clinician, stuttering support group participant, "listener" on the Internet stuttering list-serves, and researcher in stuttering, tells me there's much truth in this.

By attacking and reducing the unseen portions of fear, embarrassment, and shame that so often accompany stuttering and play a primary role in maintaining the surface symptoms of the disorder, most people who stutter are able to make great gains. Let's talk about how we can start chipping away at the iceberg. What we need are tools: icepicks, axes, and sunshine! The actual tools to melt and devour the iceberg are within our grasp. They are gifts we can give ourselves, and they include: Forgiveness, Understanding, Courage and Patience.

Forgiveness: We who stutter are our own worst critics. We are too hard on ourselves, which is a very normal human trait. Science is still unsure what causes stuttering to begin. Much research indicates that we possess a speech production mechanism that tends to fall apart under lesser amounts of stress and communication pressure than the average speaker. Nearly everyone's speech becomes halting and broken with adequate pressure, but for us, it takes less pressure to make us stumble. We may be more sensitive and susceptible to communication pressures. So let's start by forgiving ourselves for stuttering just as others must forgive themselves for perceived shortcomings. While we will probably always have to live with the tendency to have our speech fragment into stuttering, there's much we can do to minimize its effects. Secondly, let's be willing to forgive ourselves when we occasionally fail in our attempts to make changes. Making changes in our stuttering behaviors isn't easy: otherwise, we wouldn't still be stuttering! We will encounter setbacks. We may run away or lapse instinctually back into our old behavior patterns, but let's view these as opportunities to learn, to evaluate, and to develop strategies for how to do things more constructively the next time, rather than concluding with a failure and setting the stage for yet another failure in the future.

...view setbacks as opportunities to learn...

Understanding: We need to understand ourselves and our listeners. We need to understand that our own beliefs about stuttering are very different from those held by people who don't stutter. To us, stuttering is something embarrassing, humiliating, and even shameful; to the average person who doesn't stutter, however, it's often little more than noticing that we're having a terrible time talking.

Why is this? It's human nature to fear and want to avoid anything negative that makes us appear "different" or "flawed" or obviously "less able." Stuttering carries negative connotations for us because everyone else we know seems to be able to speak easily. Even children can say what they want to without fear, so there must be something wrong with us. Our reasoning isn't helped by what we see in the media, where stuttering is used to indicate character flaws such as indecisiveness, cowardice, or even worse, psychopathology or criminal deviancy. It's rare to find a heroic stutterer in print or movies!

But it's important to remember that we notice such things because we stutter ourselves; the average non-stutterer is pretty oblivious to such connotations. It's important to remember that the flaw is much more visible and significant to the person carrying it than to anyone else, just as it is to the insecure fashion model who can somehow find all kinds of facial and figure imperfections in herself and can't believe that others find her beautiful. Or, the analogy of a pimple that appears on our face during our teenage years: to us, it's huge and eye-catching and we're sure everyone is staring at it. But, in reality, few people ever notice it. Simply put, stuttering isn't that important to most people who don't stutter! We're a heck of a lot more embarrassed and concerned about it than they are.

We need to understand the reactions of others. Most normally fluent talkers know very little about stuttering, and come across it very infrequently. If we're having a "killer block" it may catch them by surprise, and generate the responses that we've come to fear. But generally, those impaired souls, whose own self-image is so poor that they must ridicule others' weaknesses to make themselves feel better, are few and far between. Most people would love to help us if they only knew what to do. When people learn that I'm a speech-language pathologist who specializes in stuttering, I'm almost immediately asked the question, "I've got a friend who stutters. When he stutters, should I finish the word for him if he can't seem to get it out, or should I just wait?" Listeners can tell when we're feeling awkward and embarrassed. They don't know what to do, and this ultimately leads to awkwardness and embarrassment on both sides.

We sense another horribly failed attempt at communication, and the iceberg of hidden hurt feelings and failure continues to grow. A

Openness lets in the sunlight that melts the iceberg.

little education on our part can make a big difference. Being open about our stuttering, and explaining it when it occurs, often opens the door to questions and dissipates the awkwardness and embarrassment on both sides. This generally results in a greatly improved communication interaction in the future. Openness lets in the sunlight that melts the iceberg, rather than keeping it hidden in the bitterly cold darkness that only helps it grow.

Courage: The greatest enemy to stuttering is courage. Stuttering thrives on our fears and failures, and stuttering wins every time we meet someone and immediately start playing the game "hide the stutter." I've done this, and I'll bet that you've probably played the game yourself: substituting words, changing what you're saying, not saying everything you want to say, and using all those little tricks you've learned to "disguise" your stuttering. We've all done these things in the vain hope of keeping this person from finding out the shameful and horrible truth that we stutter. Of course, it's not shameful and horrible to them; that connotation is primarily in **our** minds. If we are successful, because we have hidden it and they didn't catch on, what have we won? Nothing, because we're then forced to continue playing the game on every meeting with this person until the truth is at last revealed. Unfortunately, the pressure increases each time we do this. Hiding the stuttering means surrendering to the fear and shame, and this seems only to feed the cold darkness.

The problem of stuttering is complicated by the fact that our actions are in large part a normal part of human nature. It's natural to avoid unpleasant and painful things, and in the short term this is much easier than facing the unpleasantness. Psychologists talk about the primitive "fight or flight" reaction exhibited when we perceive danger (increased heart rate and blood pressure, adrenaline flooding our bloodstream.) This originally developed in prehistoric times to give us extra strength to fight our predators or extra speed to run away. Many persons who stutter exhibit these symptoms when facing difficult speaking situations that we've come to anticipate as difficult and apt to elicit large amounts of stuttering. All too often we select the "flight" response, and attempt to evade and run away from the stuttering, using all our tricks and subterfuge to avoid stuttering. When this happens, stuttering wins once again, and it grows still colder and darker inside.

What types of courage do we need to fight the darkness? Rather than running away, we can begin by acknowledging and facing our stuttering. In this book, you'll read about lots of techniques for this. Personally, I use the following three strategies fairly regularly.

Self-Identification. One way of quickly ending the game of "hide the stuttering" is to let the listener know that we stutter at the earliest convenience. Stuttering is now out in the open, and this generally removes a tremendous amount of pressure. If we do have some dysfluencies the listener knows what's happening, but neither of us has to worry about what the other person is thinking. The listener knows we are comfortable enough with it to talk about it, and we know the listener realizes what is happening. More often than not, we've reduced the pressure enough so that we end up talking pretty fluently.

Voluntary Stuttering. We need to be willing to deliberately stutter, especially by feigning a stutter when we wouldn't normally stutter on a word. This demonstrates an incredible amount of courage: we have faced and done the thing we fear the most. Moreno, we are doing the thing that the majority of our activity and efforts are spent trying to avoid. We no longer have to do those things. How incredibly liberating! We can for once look at our stuttering out in the bright sunlight, not when in a typical state of panic when the moment of real stuttering is upon us, and when our views of are anything but rational. Instead, we can now pay attention to our listeners, and to the outside world, and see their reaction in a more realistic light. They don't seem appalled or frightened, but rather curious or even attempting to be encouraging. But what's best is that we have once again stopped playing the "hide the stutter" game. Stuttering is out in the open; the game is over.

Play With Our Stuttering—voluntarily. This takes the concept of voluntary stuttering one step further. When we "play" with our stuttering, we are proving to ourselves that it isn't this horrible and shameful thing, and more importantly, that it no longer possesses any power over us. Personally, I play with my stuttering by doing lots of feigned stuttering, being much more dysfluent than normal. I try all kinds of stuttering, with my typical avoidance behaviors tossed into the mixture. I may try to actually stutter, purposefully saying those words I often tend to avoid by substitutions or disguised stuttering. On a few occasions **during therapy**, I and another person who stutterers have deliberately unleashed the most unusual and noticeable stuttering behaviors we could create on an unsuspecting listener, trying to see who could be first to make the listener "flinch."

All three techniques reduce the fear and let in the sunlight. They help to melt the iceberg. Each one takes a lot of courage to employ, for we're going against our natural instincts. On the other hand, for years we're tried following our natural instinct to run away, and that obviously hasn't helped. Maybe it's time to try the "fight" rather than "flight" part of the reflex.

Patience: Remember, Rome wasn't built in a day, and the feelings and fears that have taken years to develop into that giant underwater iceberg won't disappear in a few days or weeks. What is encouraging and exciting, however, is how fast those feelings and fears change once we start to expose and challenge them. It's easy and very human to be overwhelmed by the immensity of attacking our stuttering, but remember, the longest and most important journeys begin with a single step, and that's all we need to worry about taking right now. Make up your mind to make just one small change today.

Chapter **22**

finding your own path without professional help

Walter H. Manning

"In the hour of adversity be not without hope
For crystal rain falls from black clouds."

PERSIAN POEM

Because stuttering is a complex and uniquely human problem, change is often an arduous and lengthy process. Once a person has stuttered through the years of adolescence, the odds are slim that the disorder will go away. After stuttering for several decades, you are likely to have become a sophisticated traveler in the culture of stuttering. You will probably always be someone who stutters—more or less, harder or easier. Accepting this fact is the essential first step in beginning to change the handicapping effects of your speech.

> It really is possible to make dramatic changes.

Now for some better news. It really is possible, even if you stutter severely, to make dramatic changes, both in your speech and your response to the stuttering experience. You can learn how to use your speech production system more efficiently, you can learn to stutter in much better ways, and you can learn to live without the omnipresent fear of stuttering guiding your choices. These changes will occur sooner and more completely if you have the assistance of a good speech-language pathologist who is genuine, enthusiastic, emphatic, and sometimes demanding. But even without formal treatment there is evidence indicating that these changes can and do take place.

Just as experienced professionals adapt treatment approaches for each client, you must find your own path through the obstacles presented by stuttering. If there is an advantage to working on the problem on your own, this may be it: by following some investigation on your part, you will be able to select from the many strategies and associated techniques, those that are best for your needs. Regardless of the path you choose, it will be critical to ask yourself if you are truly ready to begin this trek for it will take a serious commitment on your part.

Getting yourself "unstuck" from stuttering will take more than changing your way of speaking. In order to lessen the handicapping effects of your situation, you must also alter many habitual ways of thinking about yourself and your stuttering, especially your pattern of making decisions based on the possibility of stuttering. Make no mistake, stuttering for adults is a multidimensional problem that requires more than a simple and passing response.

> Stuttering is a multidimensional problem.

My suggestions for you would be influenced by my understanding of your story. I would like to sit by your side and learn about your history, your motivation, and your readiness for change at this point in your life. It would be good if I had some sense about how much you need to be desensitized to stuttering. I would see if you could follow my model and voluntarily put some easy stuttering in your mouth. We would experiment with your speech and see if you are willing to vary and play with your stuttering.

Because I can't do these things I must offer a more generic list of suggestions, any one of which may or may not be the best suggestion for you at this time. I don't have *the* answers to *your* problem. As a matter of fact, I would suggest that you beware of anyone who tells you that they do. What I can offer are possible responses to your situation and you will have to select the ones that are best for you at a particular time.

The following suggestions are based both on my adventures in successfully changing my own attitudes and speech over many years and from my professional experience of working with many children, adolescents, and adults who also stutter. They are listed in five sections.

Prime Directives

Often, when I am searching for the next best step during the treatment process, I come back to three basic concepts.

- **Do not avoid.** To the best of your ability, decrease your avoidance of sounds, words, people, speaking situations, and everything else. When you avoid something, the fear increases. Each time you choose to approach something the fear tends to decrease. This will take a long time (months or years) but try to gradually decrease your reflexive response to avoid things because of the *possibility* of stuttering.

- **Speak easily.** If you are speaking and not stuttering, slightly slow your rate of speech and see if you can make your movements from one sound and word to another easily. See if you can make your speech more than just "not stuttered" but truly smooth and flowing. Begin to appreciate how easy and smooth speech can feel both physically and emotionally. If you are speaking and stuttering, do it easier and slower, at least a little. Give yourself permission to speak and stutter smoothly and easily rather than fighting through each stuttered moment.

- **Take as many speech and non-speech risks as you can.** If you can, do this with a buddy; if you can't, do it anyway.

Change The Features Under The Surface

Although these features are not easily observed by others, changing them is critical for long term success. This requires you to consider your general attitudes about life and what you tell yourself about the stuttering experience.

- Make a list of things you "Do because you stutter." These are the decisions you make because you stutter or might stutter. (e.g., Because I may stutter...I don't ask questions at a meeting. I don't always order what I want in a restaurant.

I don't make difficult telephone calls. I don't introduce myself.) Hint: This will be a much longer list than you think.

- Take risks and "push the envelope" of your speaking and non speaking activities. Try adventures that you've always thought about and wanted to do. Hint: Search for activities that seem just a half step beyond your present ability.
- Find a local stuttering support group and attend at least six meetings. The support of others who stutter is essential, and the value of support groups cannot be emphasized enough. (See the suggestions and resource information in Appendix A.)
- Read a book about stuttering written by someone who stutters.
- Tell at least one friend about your own experiences as a person who stutters. See if you can come up with humorous events, (reactions of listeners, embarrassing experiences in school) that have occurred because of your stuttering.
- Let your parents know that they didn't cause your stuttering.
- Study literature and video tapes discussing the nature and treatment of stuttering.
- Lurk and take part on Internet discussion groups focusing on stuttering. (Appendix A.)

Change The Surface Behavior of Stuttering

The surface behaviors of stuttering are those actions that we (and others) can see and hear when we stutter. The secret to changing these behaviors is not to try to stop doing them but to slightly change and vary them. Practice staying in the stuttering moment, playing with different behaviors, and, as strange as it may sound, try to have fun stuttering in different, creative ways.

- Make a map of your stuttering. Construct a list (or a drawing) of "Things I do when I stutter." Use audio or video tapes to capture samples of your speech on the telephone or talking to a friend. Analyze these tapes to see how many behaviors you can identify. Hint: As you analyze the tapes, pantomime your speech to get a feel for what you are doing when you stutter.
- Learn as much as you can about the anatomy and physiology of the speaking mechanism. Contact the Stuttering Foundation for individuals who can send you recommended sources of information.
- Learn as much as you can about the basic sound categories of speech production and how they are produced.

- Practice saying words (especially your feared words) with good airflow, gradual onset of your vocal cords, light articulatory contacts, and smooth movements, as you make the transition from one sound and syllable to another.

- Learn to differentiate (especially by feel) between constricted, tight, and hard ways of stuttering and open, smooth, and easy stuttering. You are a person who stutters, so why not learn to do it well? The quality of your stuttering is so much more important than the quantity.

- Practice varying your secondary stuttering behaviors. Come up with creative ways to alter (not stop) your old, reflexive, habitual pattern of stuttering. Change everything you can (e.g., eye and head movements, facial motions, the use of articulatory postures).

- See if you can gradually alter your use of "junk words"—those extra words that you may insert in order to postpone or time the production of a feared word that is coming along in the sentence ("Ah," "You know," "Let me see.") Hint: Each time you find yourself saying a junk word, say the word again on purpose several additional times while reading or during a conversation with a friend.

Deal with the Possibility of Relapse

Relapse is a common problem for adults following treatment. Additional individual or group treatment is often a wise choice.

- Be patient with yourself. During some days and events you will have much better success using your modification techniques.

- Even as you feel capable of achieving fluency, add some easy voluntary stuttering to your speech, especially during easy speaking situations. Prescribe this activity for yourself especially if you feel that you are beginning to use avoidance behaviors.

- Advertise your stuttering (tell people that you are a person who stutters, wear a T-shirt or button from a support group, voluntarily stutter during a conversation or a presentation) in order to release the pressure of achieving perfect fluency.

- Find a buddy to call when you are experiencing a difficult time about your stuttering (frustration, shame, embarrassment, lack of motivation).

- Locate groups such as Toastmasters where you can obtain public speaking experience.
- Consult with a local speech-language pathologist who specializes in fluency disorders. This could open the door for informal consulting, provide a source for additional materials, or even create the possibility of formal treatment.

Decide if You are Making Progress

It is important to realize that change is a process that usually is cyclical rather than linear. It often takes many efforts in approaching a complex problem before changes are seen.

- Do your best to keep from chasing the "fluency god." Some stuttering, especially if it is easy and flowing, is good.
- Don't be discouraged about temporary failures to reach your goals. You may have to go back to an earlier level of change.
- Recognize the little victories that you achieve and reward yourself for your accomplishments (e.g., using feared words, easier stuttering, taking part in new activities).
- As you decease your avoidances, recognize that a temporary increase in stuttering is likely to occur. This should be seen as a real indication of progress if you are taking more risks and living your life with greater freedom.
- As you are able to achieve some distance and mastery over your problem, recognize and appreciate the many humorous events that often accompany stuttering situations.
- Appreciate that, despite stuttering, you are entering into more speaking situations than before. It may be that you are a more social person than you realized.
- Understand that others are adjusting to your altered view of yourself and your fluency. As you change, others may also have to adjust and alter their roles.
- Appreciate that, even though you may stutter in a given situation, you are feeling less shame and embarrassment.
- Appreciate that you now initiate conversations and speak for yourself on more occasions than in the past.
- Recognize that you are considering educational, vocational, and social options that you would never have seriously considered before.
- Realize that stuttering, in some ways at least, can be regarded

as a gift, that allows you to understand yourself and others in ways that you might not have otherwise.

Conclusion

Acceptance, hope, and taking action are essential to change. The process of change is not an easy one and sometimes it will feel like the path is mostly uphill. But remember that every difficult journey can become an adventure that is fun and exciting. Changing your attitudes and behaviors associated with stuttering is a process of growth in many good ways. As you push he envelope of your speech and yourself, you will discover many new possibilities. But you are not alone on your journey. You will find many wonderful new friends, especially as you join with your fellow travelers who are members of a stuttering support group.

Chapter 23

guidelines

Paul E. Czuchna

By the time most stutterers become adults they have become profoundly frustrated in their efforts to speak fluently, and irritated at themselves for their failure to do so. They feel that they have at least average intelligence, but have endured endless labor and energy expended during their efforts to communicate. They feel helpless about mastering their stuttering and wonder what is wrong with them. As a result, they fear stuttering more and more and enjoy speaking less and less.

For years most adult stutterers have received well meaning suggestions that have been directly or indirectly aimed at stopping the stuttering altogether. These suggestions imply miraculously quick cures and fluent speech. "Take a deep breath before a word on whicih you may stutter, then say it without stuttering." "Think of what you're going to say before you say it, and you won't have any trouble," etc.

You, like every other stutterer, have heard such prescriptions that imply and instill within him the belief that it is "wrong" to stutter. In his efforts to speak fluently, the stutterer becomes more and more fearful of being unable to cope with the intermittent stuttering that may occur. The more he struggles to avoid possible stuttering or attempts to hide or disguise the stuttering that cannot be avoided, the more he denies that he has a problem.

There appear to be two main types of stutterers: (1) the *covert* stutterer who attempts to avoid contacts with feared words and situations that might identify him as a possible stutterer to his listeners and (2) the *overt* stutterer who struggles laboriously through word after word as he communicates. Which one are you?

Let us look at some of the communicative behavior of the *covert* stutterer and some of his associated feelings. Covert stutterers scan ahead during their utterances and continuously look for any expected word difficulty that might result in stuttering. They must be fully and constantly prepared for any emergency so they can avoid these words and not unmask themselves. When they anticipate possible stuttering they attempt to avoid direct contact with feared words. They postpone words they must say by various means until they feel they might be able to utter them more fluently. Or, at the precise moment they must utter a particular word, they use various timing devices such as eye blinks, quick body movements or gestures. Rather than endure any obvious struggle that might be interpreted as stuttering, they may attempt to get others to fill in these "key words" for them or completely give up their intent to communicate. Covert stutterers have learned which kinds of speaking situations tend to produce unavoidable stuttering and they have become masters at avoiding these situations (i.e., walking a mile or two to talk to someone rather than use the telephone; sending others on errands which involve speaking, etc.). Do you do these things?

In contrast, the more *overt* stutterer seemingly "barrels on through" words and sounds quite directly when he expects difficulty during his communication. He may not like his struggling efforts, but he has learned to endure them. At the same time he may have a minimum of word and situation avoidance since he expects to stutter anyway. He may, however, postpone word utterances and do some avoiding of his more obnoxious behaviors *during* moments of outward stuttering. These stutterers sense the penalty they receive from listeners who become impatient due to the amount of time it takes to communicate. Yet they still like to talk and do so. They resnt other people filling in words for them or attempting to complete their utterances. These stutterers are often profoundly frustrated in their efforts to increase their rate of speaking, yet at the same time they exhibit many kinds of struggling behaviors that really interfere with accomplishing this. They stutter harder than they need to! They do things that actually prevent them from saying their words easily. Perhaps you do, too.

Stutterers do not need to learn how to speak fluently. They already know how to do this even though they rarely pay any attention to their fluent utterances. They may have to learn more about how to respond to the fear or experience of blocking, but they do not have to learn (as something new) to say words fluently. Some of the intense frustration comes from knowing how to say words fluently, yet finding themselves stuck and unable to do so. Stutterers need to learn what to do when they do stutter if they are to eventually reduce the fear and frustration involved. As a tenative reachable goal to shoot for, they must learn to move more easily through stuttered words rather than recoiling from them. They need other choices of ways to stutter when they expect to stutter as well as other ways of completing word utterances after they block.In short, they first need to learn a better way of stuttering, one which will interfere very little with communication. Do you know how to stutter fluently?

Most stutterers initially react with revulsion and rejection to the thought of learning to stutter differently with less struggle. After all, they have spent many years attempting either not to stutter at all, or attempting to hide stuttering when it does occur. The more *covert* stutterer may respond with extreme fear and panic even to the thought of trying to learn to stutter fluently, for he has spent considerable time and effort developing his many tricks to avoid ever being discovered as being a stutterer. The *overt* stutterer may have grave doubts that he can ever learn to stutter more effortlessly, yet recognize that this would provide some relief for him. Nevertheless, the thought of learning to stutter more fluently, as an intermediate goal to shoot for, begins eventually to become a possibility. They would prefer to have a quick cure; perhaps if they could learn to be fluent even when they do stutter, it wouldn't be so bad. How do you respond to this?

The *covert* stutterer has a longer way to go than does the more overt stutterer. The covert stutterer must first literally rediscover what he is fearful of doing by deliberately stuttering more overtly when he anticipates stuttering. To do so, he must resist using his old avoidance tricks when he expects to stutter. He must learn to endure by experiencing what he is usually only guessing he might do. The *overt* stutterer, on the other hand, must learn to examine and tolerate more and more of what he actually does when he stutters rather than deny the existence of his obvious stuttering behavior. Both overt and covert stutterers must come to know vividly what is to be changed and get a fairly clear picture of the procedures that will create a more fluent kind of stuttering. They must then learn to build solid bridges to fluency rather than repeatedly trying to jump to fluency and falling and failing. Do you know how to get out of the mess where you now are?

The following crucial experiences, which you must seek again and again, are the basic building materials and equipment needed to build a bridge from where you are now to where you want to be in the future:

1. You are basically responsible for your own behavior, including your stuttering.

2. Stuttering can be deliberately endured, touched, maintained and studied.

3. Avoidance only increases fear and stuttering, and must be reduced.

4. Struggling, hurried escape from stuttering blockages, and recoiling away from expected or felt blockings, make stuttering worse than it need be, and tends to make it persist.

5. Is it possible to release yourself voluntarily from blocking or repeating prior to completing a word utterance.

6. When a moment of stuttering occurs it can be studied, and its evil effects erased as much as possible.

7. Attending to your normal speech and adopting short, forward-moving, effortless moments of stuttering reduces more severe stuttering.

8. The self-suggestion of incoming stuttering can be resisted and words can be spoken fairly normally.

9. It is possible to build barriers to destructive listener reactions that tend to precipitate stuttering.

10. Ambivalence, anxiety, guilt and hostility can be decreased.

11. Every effort should be made to build up your ego strength, self-confidence and self-respect.

12. Society in general rewards the person who obviously confronts and attempts to deal with his stuttering.

13. It is more personally rewarding to stutter fluently than to stutter grotesquely, and it is fun to be able to talk anywhere even if you do stutter.

Will you merely read this list and then forget it? Or will you consider each item carefully and see if you can find some way to use it to help yourself?

These experiences which the stutterer must repeatedly undergo may be difficult to devise or to carry out by the stutterer alone. The stutterer feels in enough lonely isolation with his stuttering problem as it is. Therapy for stutterers ordinarly requires having a competent speech therapist available as a guide, one who can share experiences with the stutterer throughout the course of therapy. The companionsh of a competent speech therapist is usually essential for therapy success. Get help if you can, but if none is available, help yourself. Others have done so!

Chapter 24

knowledge, understanding, and acceptance

Robert W. Quesal

Although I cannot speak for all stutterers, I can speak from personal experience. My experiences and yours may be considerably different, so consider my comments as things to ponder: suggestions and perspectives gained by someone who has stuttered for over four decades.

We probably do have some things in common, however. I read the first edition of *Advice To Those Who Stutter* in 1973 after ordering it from an ad I saw in *Reader's Digest*. Reading *Advice To Those Who Stutter* was a turning point in my life. I hope, after reading this chapter and the other chapters in this book, you will be helped in the way that I was.

The authors in the first *Advice To Those Who Stutter* "spoke to me" like no one had before. Before that time, I didn't know many stutterers, and no one said much about my stuttering. Most of what I "knew" about stuttering was based upon my experiences and feelings. I was trying to understand my stuttering, but I was doing it alone. The authors helped me realize that many other people shared similar experiences. Before reading that book, for example, I thought that no one else would change their order in a restaurant based upon how "easy" something was to say, or would avoid the telephone, or would wander around a store looking for something rather than asking a sales clerk, or would avoid (or leave) situations in which they would be asked to say their name. These things, which I often did, were fairly common "coping behaviors" among the stutterers whose chapters I read some 25 years ago. I was also impressed that all of the authors had become successes in life in spite of (or perhaps in some cases because of) their stuttering.

Until that time, I was living a fairly aimless existence. I had completed two years of college, but had quit school after my sophomore year. I spent part of the next year sharing an apartment with a high-school friend who was attending college in Texas. I didn't work while I was in Texas, but instead spent my days reliving the past and thinking about my future. What was I going to do? What did the future hold for a stutterer like me?

My copy of *Advice To Those Who Stutter* arrived in Texas at a most opportune time. While I was pondering what I was going to do with my life, I had the opportunity to read about the experiences of other stutterers, most of whom had become successes in the profession of speech pathology. I realized that speech pathology was a reasonable choice for my college major.

Speech pathology proved to be a perfect choice for me, and my grades improved considerably. I enjoyed my classes, I was in an environment where my stuttering may have been more accepted than in some other places, and at the same time I was in therapy for my speech. Ultimately, my speech improved, I earned bachelor's and master's degrees from Indiana University, and a Ph.D. from the University of Iowa, where I was lucky enough to study with Dean Williams, one of the authors from the original book. I can honestly say that this book turned my life around. Nearly everything I am today, as far as my speech and my professional life is concerned, can be directly traced to when I read *Advice To Those Who Stutter* in 1973.

What can I say that will be as helpful to you today as that book was to me in 1973? Over the years, I have come to believe that three things are important if we are going to come to grips with our stuttering. Those three things are **knowledge**, **understanding**, and **acceptance**. I think all these things go together, and I think those are the tools that a stutterer needs if he or she is going to be able to deal with stuttering.

Words like knowledge, understanding, and acceptance, are like many other words: they're used a lot and can have a number of different meanings. Let me provide some dictionary definitions to clarify what the terms mean to me:

Knowledge:

- Acquaintance with facts, truths, or principles as from study or investigation.
- Acquaintance or familiarity gained by sight, experience, or report.

Understanding:

- Mental process of a person who comprehends; comprehension; personal interpretation.
- Knowledge of, or familiarity with, a particular thing; *skill in dealing with or handling something* (italics added).

Acceptance:

- Regarding as proper, usual, or right.
- Enduring patiently, with resignation and tolerance.
- Favorable reception; approval; favor.

The definitions I have emphasized suggest that knowledge, understanding, and acceptance gradually evolve in an informal, rather than a formal way. I also emphasize these because even though I have studied stuttering in a formal way, much of what I now know about my own stuttering has resulted from my experiences and things that I have tried on my own. I have had the good fortune to be able to integrate my education and my experience. Knowledge, understanding, and acceptance are not linear. That is, acquiring knowledge does not mean one will acquire understanding or acceptance of stuttering. The three are interrelated.

There are a number of ways, both formal and informal, to learn about stuttering. You can learn a lot from going to therapy with a speech-language pathologist who is knowledgeable about stuttering. However, even if you can't attend formal therapy, there are numerous sources of information about stuttering that are available to you. You will learn a lot from reading this book and other resources listed in Appendix A. Another good source of information about stuttering may be a self-help group in your area.

Remember, however, that not all the information that is available about stuttering is good information. In other words, the mere fact that someone says something or writes something doesn't necessarily mean that it's true. The people who talk or write about stuttering have a particular perspective, usually based on their own unique experiences, so those perspectives may vary widely. Also, I would avoid anyone who claims to have "the answer" or "the cure" for stuttering. Consider everything that you read or hear in the context of your own experience. Delve more deeply into those aspects of stuttering that have the most relevance for you; spend less time on those things that do not relate to your experiences with stuttering.

It may be that you already know a lot about your stuttering, at least the knowledge defined above as "acquaintance or familiarity gained by sight, experience, or report." But you may want to ask yourself, "how much do I **really** know?" In other words, is your knowledge based on *reality* or is it based upon what you *think* is going on? Do you avoid certain sounds, words, situations and people, etc. because you "know" that you will stutter in that situation?

How do you know? How long has it been since you have tried to speak in those situations? How long has it been since you have said those words? Have you said the words fluently at times, but only remember the times when you have stuttered?

These questions are not meant to imply that you don't know the answers to these things, but these are the kinds of "tough questions" that we have to ask ourselves if we are truly to know about our stuttering. We need to take the time to thoroughly analyze how we talk, how we stutter, and how our stuttering varies. Perhaps just as important is to focus on those things we do *well*—how do we talk when we are more fluent? We often base our self-evaluations on how we *feel* rather than on how we actually *talk*. We may feel uncomfortable when speaking, and assume that our listener feels the same way. If we feel badly about a situation, we think that our speech was bad. Or we focus on our feelings, and want to rush through our blocks or "force words out." Many of these things may be counterproductive, but unless we spend the time studying ourselves as speakers, we never know, for sure, if they help or hinder.

The more we learn about stuttering, the better we understand how we speak and how we stutter. I don't *always* stutter when I say my name. I don't *always* have trouble when I talk to a clerk in a store. I can often say words that I thought would be difficult —perhaps not with perfect fluency, but well enough. I often can get my message across pretty well—it seems that perhaps my stuttering bothers me more than it bothers my listener.

Ah, the listener. This is a variable that is often hard to control. Some people seem pretty tolerant when we're stuttering. Others seem impatient. Others are downright nasty—they call us names, make fun of us, laugh at us. I don't find this to be a particularly enjoyable experience, and I imagine that you feel the same way. So, how do we deal with listeners? Well, this is one of the hardest things to do, but is often the most helpful: tell them that you stutter. I don't mean to go up to every person you meet and say, "Hi, I'm Bob Quesal and I stutter." But when the opportunity presents itself, make a socially appropriate comment about your stuttering.

For example, suppose you've met someone for the first time and are making small talk and you're not as fluent as you'd like to be—make a comment about your difficulty: "Gee, my stuttering seems to be pretty bad today." Or, "You'll have to forgive me, I normally don't stutter this much when I meet new people." This is what my colleague and friend Bill Murphy refers to as "normalizing" stuttering. Try to accept stuttering as part of you, like your hair color, eye color, height, athletic abilities, writing skills, and any number of other attributes.

If you are comfortable with your stuttering, your listeners will be more comfortable with it as well. Often, we think people are being cruel when they stare at us or laugh when we are having a block. Many people react that way because they don't know how to react to our stuttering. For all they know, we could be having a seizure, playing a trick on them, or something else. We often assume that our listeners should know as much about us as we know about ourselves, but that's a lot to ask. We make things easier on our listeners and ourselves when we let them know what's going on. Telling people that you stutter—normalizing your stuttering—may be one of the most difficult things to do, but it may have the biggest payback for you. It's a way to help you understand your stuttering, but more importantly, it may help others to better understand your stuttering. It also shows that you accept your stuttering, and this usually makes it easier for other people to accept it, as well.

So, take time to learn about stuttering in general, and how *you* stutter specifically. Use this knowledge to better understand yourself as a speaker and a stutterer. Try to accept stuttering as a part of you, and help others to understand and accept your stuttering. You have a lot of positive attributes. I'm sure there are things you do better than other people, there are things you know that other people don't

> Help others to understand and accept your stuttering.

know, and there are a variety of things that make you a unique individual. Your stuttering is just part of the person that you are. It doesn't define you unless you allow yourself to be defined by stuttering.

Perhaps most important is to realize that you are not in this alone. Don't be like I was and try to muddle your way through things on your own. Take advantage of everything that's out there: people, information, resources, and other sources of help. This book is a great place to start. It was for me, and I'm confident it will be for you.

Chapter 25

maintaining dignity while living with stuttering

Gary J. Rentschler

Most of us who stutter feel a strong sense of embarrassment, guilt, shame and even hostility related to the disruptions in our speech. Years of experiencing these feelings influence how we think about ourselves. Feelings of diminished self-worth, low self-esteem, inferiority, shyness and withdrawal are common among those of us who stutter.

There are those who in spite of stuttering severely, seem to enjoy life and are not diminished by their disfluent speech. These people share certain qualities which enable them to maintain the respect of others and project a strong feeling of self-worth. They are able to (1) view their stuttering objectively, (2) accept themselves with imperfections, and (3) explain their stuttering openly to others.

Dealing with Stuttering Objectively. For many of us, the negative emotions stirred during disfluent moments are so strong that we are unable to describe what happens in much detail. Some comment: "I was very nervous," or "That was really bad," while others say, "My vocal cords locked and I wasn't able to make any sound," or "My lips were pressed together with too much force." Note that the first two statements expressed the *emotion*, while the second two described the *physical charac-teristics* of what had happened. The negative emotions which develop obscure our ability to see the physical behaviors clearly and objectively, and interfere with our ability to learn more about our stuttering. Being able to see beyond our feelings requires that we distance ourselves from our stuttering in order to describe its physical characteristics. The more we know about our stuttering behaviors, the more power we gain over them and the better we will become in managing their physical and emotional components.

Accepting Ourselves. We who stutter tend to develop unrealistic expectations for the fluency of our speech. This is understandable because so much negative attention has been focused on our disfluencies that it is only natural to want to be noticed less for our shortcomings. For many of us, this negative attention generalizes into an overall dissatisfaction with ourselves as people. We become our own harshest critic and berate ourselves on many issues in addition to our stuttering.

Many people are able to see beyond their "blemishes" and accept themselves as a person with imperfections. Our parents and our friends have imperfections, but we are able to see beyond their flaws and cherish their love and fellowship in spite of their shortcomings. It is our imperfections that make us individual and memorable. To embrace our flaws is to honor our uniqueness.

Formulating an "Explanation." Part of establishing distance between ourselves and our stuttering is learning to appreciate how our listeners feel when we communicate with them. Being able to see ourselves through someone else's eyes represents another means of helping ourselves become more resilient to the negative effects of our stuttering.

Compared to obvious physical handicaps (e.g., being confined to a wheelchair), stuttering is "invisible"—at least until we speak. Consequently, listeners are caught off guard when we stutter. They have no warning or opportunity to *prepare themselves,* and may therefore be surprised by our stuttering. They feel both curiosity and surprise, and search for an explanation of what they see and hear. Many of the outward signs of stuttering can give the impression of having a seizure, muscle spasm or other medical problem. The listener becomes alarmed, confused and doesn't know how to react to stuttering.

Our intuition often tells us not to acknowledge to others that we stutter. Perhaps our strong sense of embarrassment, guilt or shame causes us to retreat within ourselves, somehow hoping that the listener hasn't noticed our effortful speaking, bodily contortions, or facial grimaces. In this instance, our intuition does not serve us well. By not acknowledging and explaining our stuttering, our listener's curiosity is heightened. As their search for an explanation continues unguided, the conclusions they reach often exceed the stigma attached to stuttering. Left to explain their observations, listeners often question the mental or physical competence of the stuttering speaker. This questioning leads to the ridicule which is so hurtful to those of us who stutter and reinforces the negative feelings about ourselves.

Most people do not intentionally ridicule persons having difficulty when an impairment is apparent. For example, when you see someone in a wheelchair struggling to open a door, your first instinct is to help them rather than laugh at them. Why? You see and **understand** their difficulty and reflexively help them. You aren't curious why they can't open the door. It's obvious—they're in a wheelchair, and so you help them by opening open the door.

Think for a minute about your reaction to this situation. A man is carrying two boxes: suddenly his body starts shaking and he drops the boxes, breaking the glassware they contain. After a minute his shaking stops, he picks up the boxes and walks away. What are your thoughts? "What's wrong with him? Maybe he is epileptic, or maybe he's really weird." Without an explanation, your curiosity is engaged, and you don't know what to think.

Now instead of walking away after the incident, what if the man said, "I've just started taking a new medication and I guess I wasn't prepared for its side effects. Can you help me sit down and get me some water?" Feel yourself change from being puzzled and curious, to being understanding and wanting to help. You become that same sensitive, kind, helping person who held open the door for the person in the wheelchair. By offering an explanation of our stuttering we change our listener from being puzzled and curious to being sensitive, kind and helpful. The *explanation* makes the difference.

An explanation might include (1) a statement of the nature of our stuttering, (2) some facts we know about it, and (3) some things others could do which we might find helpful. Let's look at some examples of how others have formulated their "explanations":

Michael B.: "I've had this stuttering problem my whole life. I often get anxious just before I speak which causes me to tense my vocal cords and no sound comes out. It takes me a little more time to say what I want to, so I hope you understand that I need to speak slowly."

Kim M.: "I get so embarrassed when my speech gets stuck in my throat. I've heard that some research is finding that people who stutter use their brain differently when they speak. I'm helping myself now by getting speech therapy. I'm sure my stuttering must make you a little uncomfortable, but I'm really fine. If you could wait an extra minute or two until I'm done it would help me out a lot."

Rob S.: "Ha! Would you listen to me? That stutter sure got the better of me that time. I'd better get 'back in the saddle' and slow myself down a bit!"

Phil R.: "As you can see, sometimes I stutter. My father stutters too. It seems that I try to get too many ideas out too quickly and get all tangled up. It's a strange and frustrating feeling. I need to focus more on slowing down and easing my words out. Let me know if I start going too quickly again."

These examples can be very helpful in explaining our stuttering to others and cultivating their understanding. In each explanation, the person acknowledges their difficulty and labels it; some refer to it as *stuttering* while others describe it more generally as a *problem speaking*. Giving it a name or label takes the mystery out of the behaviors. Identifying it helps tell what it *is* as well as what it *is not*. If it **is** a speech problem, then it **is not** a mental disorder or some sort of "weird" twitching behavior. It implicitly enables us to take responsibility for our stuttering as well. This is important because it begins the transformation from being the victim of our stuttering to empowering us to change our stuttering, eventually minimizing its effects on our speech.

Each explanation also presents some factual information about the person's speech. This reflects an objective awareness, understanding and acceptance of their stuttering. Explanations also offer the listener suggestions of how they might help. Most listeners don't have much experience with stuttering and feel awkward because they don't know what to do. When they find out, they generally do it. We've now transformed a potential critic into an important ally in helping overcome the effects of our stuttering.

Perhaps the first person, however, who deserves an explanation of their stuttering is **you**. Stuttering, feeling out of control, and not understanding why is a distressing experience. Without an explanation, these frightening feelings grow unabated. Having a rational explanation helps to stop the negative thinking and fear which exacerbate stuttering. Your personal explanation can be the basis of strength to explain your stuttering to others in an objective and dignified way. It should be more in-depth and detailed. It reflects more that you know about yourself and your stuttering.

Your personal explanation might read as follows: "I often stutter when I speak. The cause of stuttering is not yet known, but I respond to situations I feel to be stressful by tensing my vocal cords. Over the years, I have become anxious about speaking. My anxiety leads to more tension in my vocal mechanism, which results in more disfluencies. The excess tension does not enable my vocal folds to vibrate and I am unable to produce sound. Often when this happens I get embarrassed and look away from my listener. Sometimes I move my head up and down when I try to get the sound out. I find my stuttering to be very frustrating and embarrassing in that being unable to express my ideas makes me feel inferior to others."

"I am a normal person; anyone would react to this problem in the ways which I do. In learning about my stuttering I am learning about the things I do to compensate for it. Many of my reactions to my stuttering serve to make it stronger. I am learning to change some of those reactions and gain more control over my stuttering. I have been stuttering for many years and it will take a while to overcome many of the feelings that have developed. I know the situations in which I have difficulty and I have learned some ways to deal with them. I talk to myself in more positive ways and accept myself with my flaws. As I am learning to accept myself, I am learning to let people see me and accept me as a person who stutters."

These statements convey a deeper knowledge, acceptance and strength which project a sense of dignity. Perhaps these are not the words you would use, but they reflect the positive, reassuring, and self-respecting tone which leads to living peaceably with stuttering.

Conclusion. Stuttering complicates almost every aspect of our lives. The negative emotions which develop limit our participation in activities, our interactions with others and influence how we feel about ourselves. Our own imperfections are of far greater concern to us than they are to others. The ways by which we convey ourselves to others, as well as how we feel about ourselves, influence the way they respond to us. Confronting our imperfections with objectivity and accepting *all* of our many dimensions, enables us to carry ourselves with dignity. By attending to our own need to understand and accept our stuttering behaviors, we are better able to bring about the understanding and acceptance of others.

Chapter 26

your life is too important to spend it worrying about stuttering

Kenneth O. St. Louis

Dear Friend Who Stutters,

I grew up in an isolated valley in northwestern Colorado on a ranch. I had a wonderful childhood living in the country, attending a one-room schoolhouse, and interacting mostly with my cousins. But I stuttered. My family told me that my uncle, who died in a tractor accident when I was very young, had stuttered as well. Little else was said. Apparently my parents had been told by a speech therapist to ignore my stuttering. Although family, relatives, and friends accepted my stuttering, I was basically on my own.

I grew up without the benefit of effective therapy from a speech-language pathologist (SLP), and it wasn't until high school that I finally sought and received formal therapy. Thanks to that help I can now talk nearly all the time without fear and with very little stuttering. How much easier it would have been if my parents and I had access to this book and other resources that are available.

You stutter too. No doubt it bothers you or you would not be reading this book. There are more SLPs now, so maybe you have had some therapy. Maybe not. I know there are lots of places where speech therapy services are not available or folks are not aware that they are available. In many places in the world, there are no services at all. My first suggestion is to check to see if there are any stuttering self-help organizations in your area. These are organizations of stutterers who meet regularly to support one another. If not, think about starting one. It's always helpful to discover that you are not alone.

Here you are, though, looking for advice and help. Good! That's the first important step, "**locating resources**." I hope you will find a competent SLP who can help you, but this may not be possible just now. So I'd like to give you some suggestions and ways of thinking about your stuttering.

You've taken the first step. Now, let's take the second. I call it "**taking stock**." You see, as much as nearly all stutterers want help, everyone has different backgrounds, different expectations, and different levels of motivation. Helping yourself to overcome the agonizing fears of talking, learning to speak without avoiding words or situations, or finding easier ways to "stutter through" your blocks takes courage and hard work. It is not for the faint hearted. Are you ready for the work ahead? Let's see.

First, tell "your story of stuttering." Tell it in any form or sequence that comes to mind. Either write it down in journal form or tape record yourself while you are alone. (Most stutterers don't stutter very much while talking to themselves and this would be a good way for you to listen to how well you really can talk.) After you have finished this assignment, ask yourself the following questions, and write down your answers: How much has stuttering affected my life? How much time or money would I be willing to give up to improve my speech? Who would support my efforts? Who would not? What other important challenges besides my stuttering am I facing right now? What positive things are going on? What advice or therapy have I had that helped my stuttering? What didn't help? If it didn't help, how much was the fault of the advice or training and how much was my fault? What are my future prospects for getting therapy? Am I willing to tackle the very difficult problem of stuttering, even though I can't be guaranteed that I will be totally fluent?

If you answered "no" to the last question, it's not a sign of weakness or failure. I assume you have good reasons. It may simply mean that you aren't sure you can do it on your own and that you would rather seek the advice of a competent SLP who specializes in stuttering. It may also mean that your stuttering does not cause you enough discomfort to make it worth the time and hard work to improve your fluency. It may mean that your life is just too complicated right now.

If your answer was "yes," let's go on to the next step, **"reducing your burden."** Write down everything that you do, or avoid doing, when and because you stutter. Try to stick with what you actually DO, and for this assignment, don't include your attitudes or feelings. Your list should include things like: "I repeat the first sound of a hard word at least five times"; "I don't look at the person I'm talking to"; "I avoid answering the telephone"; "I often open my mouth and can't make a sound"; "I blink my eyes when I stutter." It should not include feeling statements like: "Speaking in front of a group terrifies me"; "I hate people that smile or laugh when I talk"; or "Stuttering frustrates me."

The goal of this step is to begin to see your stuttering in a new light: not something to be feared or avoided, but something that is a part of you that need not prevent you from (1) talking to whomever you want (2) whenever you want (3) about whatever you want. How in the world can you do that? There

See your stuttering in a new light.

are lots of ways, but let me suggest a few techniques. The first one is to look the listeners in the eye while you talk and make a mental note of what they are actually doing. Most listeners are puzzled or unsure how to react. Looking them in the eye while talking, surprisingly, will put them at ease.

The next technique may seem very strange and scary indeed. Start stuttering on purpose (or faking) in real speaking situations. You don't have to stutter severely. On otherwise easy words, try repeating the first sounds or syllables three or four times, or prolong (stretch out) some of the sounds for about two seconds. Compared to the rest of your stuttering, these will hardly be noticeable to your listeners. For example, you might say to someone, "Puh-puh-puh-pa-pa-uh-pardon (*real*) me, cuh-cuh-cuh-uh-c-cuh-can (*real*) you tell mih-mih-mih-me (*faked*) the time?" Pick a free day and do 10 to 20 of these. Why stutter on purpose? Because, as you will probably discover after doing numerous faked stutterings, stuttering seems less "out of control." Also, even though you recognize that you usually stutter, you always start to speak hoping that you won't. This time you know you will stutter (whether real or faked), and that makes all the difference. Suddenly—and maybe for the first time in your life—you are behaving in a way that is consistent with who you are. You are a stutterer and you stutter. Simple as that. It's like Popeye's declaration, "I yam what I yam." Practice stuttering on purpose for several days until you can do it easily.

Try faking at the end of a real stuttering instead of giving in to the tendency to rush ahead as soon as you feel the "speech flag man" wave you on after that unplanned stop. Repeat or prolong more. You don't have to enjoy it, but you can get that stuttering monkey off your back so that at least you are leading it around— not the monkey telling you where to go and what to say.

Pick a few situations where you will be talking with strangers and begin by telling them that you stutter. This may surprise you. The most disinterested of listeners will suddenly perk up and want to hear more about it. And besides being intensely interested in everything you have to say, they will be both sympathetic and impressed with your courage and forthrightness. You will probably feel less need to avoid and struggle. After all, they already know you stutter. You told them.

Do things that you typically avoid, like leaving a message on an answering machine. Go ahead and stutter, and then reward yourself by taking a walk in the park or eating a favorite food for having done it.

If you have succeeded in "reducing the burden," you are now talking more, enjoying it more, and realizing that you really do have something to say. You may also discover that stuttering was not as big a problem as you thought it was. Perhaps you are now thinking seriously about that college major or that job or career that you never let yourself contemplate. Perhaps you are finding new and exciting relationships with other people.

But you probably still stutter, even severely at times. If you are like me, you may want to be more fluent not only so that you can feel good about yourself as a speaker, but also to become a more effective communicator. If so, you're ready for the final step, "**changing the way you stutter**." I don't know how far you can go with this step on your own. You may need to see an SLP to help you change the way that you stutter to a form that satisfies you. But let me suggest some strategies that may help you become more fluent.

You probably have noticed that you don't use the old tricks, like eye blinks, head jerks, short gasps of air, or those "uh's" you use to get started as much as you did before. But it's likely that many remain, especially when you get into a hard stutter. Try to eliminate those unnecessary tricks. Talk to yourself while you watch what you do in a mirror. Talk and read while tape recording yourself and then listen to the tape. Write down all the tricks you see and hear. Then try to talk without them, but don't try not to stutter! That's very important and worth repeating. **Do not try not to stutter**! Trying not to stutter is what motivated you to acquire all those tricks in the first place. Go ahead and stutter, but *try to talk in a new way*.

If you have been able to lessen the tricks, then you might decide to press on and try to change the way that you actually stutter. Again, this is better done in therapy, but let me suggest some guidelines. Try to stutter with less tension. You may not be able to stop stuttering, but you probably can change the way that you stutter. Try using easy repetitions that are slow and even—not fast and irregular. Or try using prolongations that are smooth and unforced. Think: "Slow, smooth, and easy." In either case, it is very important that you don't hold your breath or have silent blocks. If you do, get some air and voice going before trying to modify your stuttering, even if it sounds strange. You can't modify stuttering when you're holding it in. Try to think beyond the sound or syllable you get stuck on. Think of the whole word or phrase and keep moving through the entire sequence while concentrating on smoothness, ease, and relaxation—even while stuttering. If you find yourself jerking out of a block, pause, and go back and try it again. This will certainly interrupt communication but it will let your listener know loud and clear that you are *working* on your speech and that *you* are in control.

If you are successful in using these strategies, which some SLPs refer to as "stutter more fluently" techniques, you may find that you are capable of shortening your stutters and simplifying them to the point that they hardly delay your communication.

You may find that you don't stutter as much as you used to, partly because you are not so concerned about it, but also because you have discovered that as you think about and monitor your speech, less and less stuttering occurs. It is as if you have learned to do the things with your breathing, voicing, and articulating that you would do if you did not stutter.

Finally, if you have succeeded with these steps, plan to work on your speech a little bit every week for the next several years. Old habits die hard. Stutter on purpose once in a while and practice stuttering openly and easily.

Above all, get on with your life in spite of your stuttering!

do-it-yourself kit for stutterers

Harold B. Starbuck

Dear Sir or Madam: In reply to your letter of complaint about our Do-It-Yourself Kit for Stutterers, I apologize for not including the instructions. However, the kit was supposed to be empty! You don't need any gadgets to correct your stuttering. You already have all the tools and equipment you need. As long as you've got your body, complete with movable parts, you're set to begin. Don't ever forget that even though you went to the most knowledgeable expert in the country, the correction of stuttering is still a do-it-yourself project. Stuttering is your problem. You stutter in your own unique way. The expert can tell you what to do and how to do it, but you're the one who has to do it. You're the only person on earth who can correct your stuttering. Here are your instructions:

The first thing you must become is an honest stutterer. By that I mean you've got to stop trying to be fluent. You have to stop struggling with your feared words. Go ahead and stutter on them. Let your stuttering come out into the open. Hit

> Become an honest stutterer.

the block head on and let it run its course. Start by stuttering aloud to yourself. Stutter on every word you say. Stutter two or three times on every word. Get used to it and notice that as you stutter freely you can eliminate all those retrials, avoidances, and half-hearted speech attempts. Practice on your family and friends. They won't mind and will be rooting for you. This is a tough step, but do it in every speaking situation until you are stuttering freely. Don't try to talk fluently without stuttering.

Now that you are able to stutter openly and without fear or shame, you can begin to answer the question, "How do I stutter?" You've got to examine and analyze the act of speaking to see what errors you're making. You must be making mistakes somewhere or you would be speaking fluently. What are you doing wrong that makes your speech come out as stuttering? Speech is, after all, just a stream of air we inhale, reverse, and push out our mouths while we shape and form it into speech sounds. One must realize that you can't have speech unless you have the air coming out your mouth. Examine your speech breathing. Are you inhaling a sufficient amount? After the air is in and you're ready to talk, are you reversing it smoothly and starting an outward flow, or are you holding it in your lungs? Are you blocking it off in your throat at the level of your vocal folds? (This happens on most vowel blocks.) Are you humping your tongue up in the back of your mouth and blocking it there, as on K and G? Is the tip of the tongue jammed against your gum ridge blocking the air on T and D? Have you jammed your lips together so no air can flow out on P and B? No air flow means no speech, and hard contacts between any two parts of the speech mechanism result in a blocked air stream. Now examine yourself a little more closely. Examine the muscular movements, stresses, and strains you use in producing those hard contacts. Examine the muscular tensions and pressures. Is it any wonder you stutter? Speech is an act of almost continuous movement, and when you stop that movement you're in a stuttering position. In order to say any speech sound, you have to move into position to say that sound, move through it, and then move out of it into position for the next sound. Find out what and where your blockages and stoppages are, and what muscular tension causes them.

Is there a solution? There is to every problem! What you've got to do now is to correct every problem or error you've analyzed. We call this the *Post-block Process of Correction*. Here's how it works:

Stutter on a word. When the word is completed, stop completely and analyze all of the errors you made while all the

148

tensions and pressures are still fresh. Now, figure out a correction for each error. For example, suppose the air was blocked off in your throat on a vowel sound. The correction is an open throat. You will have to concentrate on the throat area so no muscular action jams the vocal folds closed. Concentrate on keeping them open the way they were when you inhaled. Reverse the air stream slowly, start the sound, and say it.

Suppose that the lip muscles had jammed the lips shut into a hard contact which allowed no air to pass. The correction would be a light contact or, better, no contact at all between the lips. Concentrate on controlling the lip muscles so that the lips just barely touch, or almost touch, and air is able to flow between them. An important aspect here is movement out of the sound, so you have to control the lip muscles in their movement out of the sound as well as into it. The air flow must be coordinated with the lip movement so that the sound is produced as the lips form the sound.

Figure out a correction for every error as in the above examples. When you have all the necessary corrections figured out, you are ready to try the word again. Exaggerate your corrections at first when you say the word, paying more attention to how the word feels rather than to how it sounds. The sounds may be slightly distorted and prolonged at first. That's good. The prolongation is the result of slow careful muscular movements as you move into, through and out of the sounds. The distortion is the result of light loose contacts. Feel the controlled air flow; feel the controlled muscle movements as you move fluently through the word with no stoppages.

Do a good job on the Post-block Process of Correction. This is where speech correction takes place. Don't just say the words over again fluently after you stutter. Say them carefully, concentrating on the feelings of muscular action as you coordinate the breath stream with the formation of sounds. Concentrate on the feelings of movement and fluency.

In the above step, we worked on the stuttering after it happened. Now we're going to move ahead a bit and work on it while it's happening. To do this you still have to stutter. While you are stuttering (which means you've got to keep the block going longer than the average), you must analyze what is happening incorrectly. When the errors are analyzed, you can start making corrections such as stopping a tremor, loosening a contact, and getting rid of tension until you are producing the stuttered sound in a stable, correct way. Then you can initiate movement out of the sound and complete the word. We call this step the *Block Process of Correction*. You go through the same process as you did in post-block corrections, only now you should be able to do it while you are stuttering. By now you should be able to recognize your errors almost instantly and know what corrections have to be made. Make the corrections, smooth out the sound, and complete the word. Practice this on any word you say. Stutter on purpose, get it under your control, and say the word.

You've gone through the Post-block and Block Processes of Correction. Now let's work on the stuttering even earlier. Let's work on it before it ever happens. This is the *Pre-Block Process of Correction*. When you come to a word you're going to stutter on— don't! Stop just before you start that word. Analyze how you would have stuttered on it had you said that word. Figure out the needed corrections and use them, saying the word just as you would a post-block correction. Feel the movements and fluency here too. With very little practice, you can eliminate the pause period and prepare for any feared word as you approach it. Take advantage here of your anticipation, expectancy, and fear of stuttering. An excellent way to work on this process is to select any word, feared or not, figure out how you would normally stutter on it, then figure out corrections, and apply the corrections when you get to the word.

You're now using *Predetermined Speech*. You are determining beforehand what movements you have to make, and how you have to make them, in order to say sounds and words fluently. You should be speaking fluently now, but don't fall into the trap of thinking you are a normal speaker. Normal speech for you is stuttering speech. Be proud of your abnormal predetermined fluent speech. Use it. Keep up your skills of controlling your muscle movements that produce speech. You have to eliminate your errors before, or while, they are happening. Once your speech is out beyond your lips, you can't pull it back and correct it. You must monitor your speech as you are producing it. Monitor your air flow, your muscle movements as you form sounds, and your movements through and out of sounds. Feel your fluency, and don't worry about the sound. That will take care of itself if you take care of the mechanism that is producing it.

Now you know why the kit was empty!

Chapter **28**

putting it together

Charles Van Riper

Now that you have read all of these suggestions you probably have some mixed feelings of confusion, helplessness and even disappointment. Perhaps you were hoping that at least one of these stuttering experts would have found a quick, easy, magical cure for your distressing disorder. Instead, it is quite evident that no such panacea exists and that, if you want relief from your miseries, you've got to earn that relief by making some real changes in the way you react to your stuttering and to your listeners and to yourself. As Dr. Emerick says, "The first thing to do is to admit to yourself that you need to change, that you really want to do something about your stuttering." Perhaps you are willing to make that admission but have some reservations about having to do what Dr. Boehmler calls the "dirty work of therapy." Some of the suggested procedures may at the moment seem far beyond your courage or capacities. Is the pay-off worth the cost?

All these authors answer that question with a resounding yes. I know these writers. They talk well and live well. All of them were severe stutterers. All of them know from personal experience your self doubts and the difficulties of self therapy but universally they insist that you need not continue to suffer, that

*This chapter was the last in the original book *To the Stutterer*. Hence, it does not summarize those chapters added in 1998.

you can change yourself as they have changed themselves and can become fluent enough to make the rest of your life a very useful and rewarding one. Perhaps you have already had some speech therapy and have failed and so feel that nothing can be done. If so, reread what Dr. Freund has told you about the success of his own self therapy after the best authorities in Europe had treated him unsuccessfully. Or you may be feeling that you are too old to begin now. If so, read what Dr. Sheehan had to say about the 78 year old retired bandmaster. Or you may be saying that you cannot do it alone without help, yet many of the authors agree with Dr. Starbuck's statement that essentially "The correction of stuttering is a do-it-yourself project. Stuttering is your problem. The expert can tell you what to do and how to do it, but you are the one who has to do it. You are the only person on earth who can correct your stuttering." While most of these writers would prefer to have you get competent professional guidance, they do not at all feel that it is impossible for you to get real relief without it. "Get help if you can," advises Professor Czuchna, "but if not, help yourself. You can!" They would not write so earnestly if they were not sure that you can do much to solve your difficulties. Moreover, you must remember that this is not the kind of false assurance or hope that you have received from others who never stuttered. This comes straight from persons who have known your despair and lack of confidence, from stutterers who have coped successfully with the same problems that trouble you.

At the same time, and as a measure of their honesty, they are realistic. They hold out little hope for what you have long dreamed of—the complete cure. Universally, they insist or imply that you can learn to live with your stuttering and to be pretty fluent anyway. This may be hard for you to accept—as it was hard for them too. The present writer has worked with a great many stutterers and has helped most of them to overcome their handicaps but only a few of the adult ones ever become completely free from the slightest trace of stuttering in all situations always. As Dr. Sheehan, the psychologist, advises, "Don't waste your time and frustrate yourself by trying to speak with perfect fluency. If you've come into adult life as a stutterer, the chances are that you'll always be a stutterer, in a sense. But you don't have to be the kind of stutterer that you are now—you can be a mild one without much handicap." We find this thought expressed by many of the authors. Dr. Neely says, "My own experience has been that nothing 'cures' an adult stutterer, but one can effectively manage stuttering so that it ceases to be a significant problem throughout life." Dr. Murray writes, that he has known many adult stutterers who achieved a good recovery but not one who claimed to be completely free from disfluency. Throughout this book, you have read many suggestions for the modification of your stuttering, for learning to stutter in ways that permit you to be reasonably fluent and free from emotional upheaval or social penalty. If these authors have one common message to you, it is this—you can change your abnormal reactions to the threat or the experience of stuttering and when you do so, most of your troubles in communicating will vanish. Is this bad? Is this not enough? As Dr. Emerick says, we cannot promise you a rose garden, but we can offer you a much better communicative life than the fearful, frustrating one you now endure.

But you may protest that you don't know where or how to begin. If you will read this book again, you will find author after author saying that the first thing to do is to study your stuttering and its associated feeling. In this, there is remarkable agreement. As Miss Rainey, the public school speech therapist, suggested to the young man she interviewed, you should get a mirror, and a tape recorder if possible, and start observing how you stutter, perhaps as you make a telephone call while alone, so that you can know how much of your avoidances and struggle is unnecessary and only complicates your difficulty. Dr. Dean Williams and Dr. Dave Williams offer important sets of very challenging questions that you can ask yourself as you do this observing. Other authors provide other ways that you can use to study your stuttering and feelings but all of them feel that this is how you should begin.

All of us know that this process of confronting yourself will not be pleasant, but we also know you will find, as you observe and analyze what you do and feel when stuttering or expecting to stutter, that you will then know what you have to change. And will want to! Besides, isn't it about time you stopped pretending that you are a fluent speaker? Isn't it time, as Dr. Starbuck phrases it, for you "to become an honest stutterer," to come to grips with your problem, at least to look at it objectively?

To do so, you will have to accept another suggestion that these authors make almost unanimously. You've got to talk more and avoid less. You've got to start giving up what Miss Rainey called your "camouflage." We know that this too will be hard to do but over and over again you will find these writers insisting that they had to overcome their panicky need to hide their stuttering before they began to improve. They tell you, as Dr. Moses advises, to bring your stuttering into the open, to let it be seen and heard rather than concealed as though it were a dirty shameful thing rather than a problem that you are trying to solve. How can you possibly know what you have to change if you refuse to look at it? Aren't you tired to the bone of all this running away and hiding? Different authors outline different ways of decreasing this avoidance but you should be impressed by their basic agreement that you should admit, display and confront your stuttering openly and objectively.

There is another point on which almost all of them also agree. It is that you can learn to stutter much more easily than you now do and that when you master this, you will be able to speak very fluently even if you may continue to stutter occasionally. As Dr. Sheehan says, "You can stutter your way out of this problem." The idea—that it is unnecessary to struggle when you feel blocked and that there are better ways of coping with the experience—may seem very strange at first, but if this book holds any secret for successful self therapy, it lies here. These writers say it in different ways. Dr. Emerick describes the process as getting rid of the excess baggage, the unnecessary gasps and contortions and recoils. In his account of his own self therapy, Dr. Gregory tells how he experimented with different ways of stuttering before he overcame his fear of it. Other authors tell you to learn to stutter slowly and easily. What they all seem to be saying is that it is possible to stutter in a fashion which will impair your fluency very little. Indeed, Dr. Murray suggests that if you study your stuttering, you will find that you already have some of these short, easy moments of stuttering in your speech and that if you will recognize them, they can serve as goals. If you read this article again, you will find him saying, "If you can learn to whittle the others down to similar proportions, most of your scoreable difficulty will have disappeared" and that "there are countless ways in which to stutter. You have a choice as to how you stutter even though you may not have a choice as to whether or not you'll stutter." Along with other authors, Dr. Agnello says that you should try different ways of stuttering, that you need not remain "bound" to your old patterns of stuttering. The present writer, now sixty-seven years old, agrees. For years he tried to keep from stuttering and only grew worse. Not until he found that it was possible to stutter easily and without struggling did he become fluent. He was born at the age of thirty years and has had a wonderful life ever since. How old are you?

So we suggest that you reread this book, this time to work out the design of your own self therapy. Your stuttering won't go away. There are no magical cures. You will not wake up some morning speaking fluently. You know in your heart that there is work to be done and that you must do it. This book contains many suggestions, and many guidelines. Your job is to sort out and organize those that seem appropriate to your own situation, to devise a plan of self therapy that fits your needs, and then begin the changing that must take place. Why spend the rest of your life in misery?

appendix a

Initially, we considered trying to provide a comprehensive listing of the names, addresses and contact information for the numerous helpful resources that are available. It soon became apparent that this would be an impossible task because there are so many. And even if we could generate such a list, it would soon be obsolete due to changes in the addresses and phone numbers. Consequently, we are limiting our resource list to just two sources. Each of the sources listed can serve as a powerful link to other sources of information. From these resources, you will find a link to the dozens of local, state, national and international resources and self-help groups that are available to you, as well as to internet, listserv and e-mail resources.

The Stuttering Foundation

Address:　　3100 Walnut Grove Rd., Suite 603
　　　　　　Memphis, TN 38111-0749

Phone:　　　800/992-9392　　　　　Facsimile: 901/452-3931

e-mail:　　　info@stutteringhelp.org

Web Site:　　www.stutteringhelp.org
　　　　　　www.tartamudez.org

Synopsis:　　The Stuttering Foundation has extensive information on topics such as prevention, early intervention, and therapy for stuttering as well as the latest information about basic research on stuttering; twenty-eight books and thirty-seven videotapes and DVDs on stuttering, a worldwide referral list of speech-language pathologists who specialize in stuttering; information about support groups in the U.S., Canada, and around the world; numerous annual workshops on stuttering for speech-language pathologists; nineteen brochures on the topic; and a quarterly Newsletter.

　　　　　　The Stuttering Foundation Web site gives information on brochures, referral lists, services provided by the Foundation, educational information, videotapes, publications, information about the Foundation itself, links to other Web sites that deal with stuttering, and information telling how to access listservs devoted to stuttering. It also has essays, stories, articles and case histories written by people who stutter as well as by clinicians.

The Stuttering Homepage

Web Site: www.mnsu.edu/comdis/kuster
(Judy Kuster, Web Weaver)

Synopsis: This Homepage provides links to other Web Sites that deal with stuttering, as well as information telling how to access listservs devoted to serving: STUTT-L, STUT-HLP and STUTT-X. There is also information pertaining to topics such as: prevention, early intervention and therapy for stuttering; information about support organizations; a "bookstore" section with references to printed information about stuttering; essays/stories, case studies; as well as research information, etc. Also of interest are links that are "Just for Kids" and "Just for Teens."

616.8554 Adv

Advice to those who stutter